THE UNPOPULAR ONES

FIFTEEN AMERICAN MEN AND WOMEN WHO STOOD UP FOR WHAT THEY BELIEVED IN

Jules Archer
History for Young Readers

THE UNPOPULAR ONES

FIFTEEN AMERICAN MEN AND WOMEN
WHO STOOD UP FOR WHAT THEY
BELIEVED IN

JULES ARCHER

Foreword by Kathleen Krull

Sky Pony Press
NEW YORK

Historical texts often reflect the time period in which they were written, and new information is constantly being discovered. This book was originally published in 1968, and much has changed since then. While every effort has been made to bring this book up to date, it is important to consult multiple sources when doing research.

Visit our website at www.skyponypress.com.

10 9 8 7 6 5 4 3 2 1

Library of Congress Cataloging-in-Publication Data is available on file.

Series design by Brian Peterson
Cover photo credit Associated Press

PICTURE CREDITS
Brown Brothers, 85, 109, 146-147; Culver Pictures Inc., 22, 47, 80, 120, 155; Historical Pictures Service—Chicago, 12, 34, 64, 74, 90, 102, 115, 129, 135; United Press International, 126, 163, 179, 187.

Print ISBN: 978-1-63450-200-9
Ebook ISBN: 978-1-63450-899-5

Printed in the United States of America

To August Lenniger
for the past twenty-five years

CONTENTS

FOREWORD   ix

INTRODUCTION   xiii

1 "Newe and Dangerous Opinions"
   ROGER WILLIAMS   I

2 Morning Star of Liberty
   JOHN PETER ZENGER   11

3 "Whether It Be Popular Or Unpopular"
   THOMAS PAINE   21

4 The Common Scold
   ANNE ROYALL   33

5 The Beatnik of 1830
   JOSEPH PALMER   45

6 "Burn the Tribune! Hang Old Greeley!"
   HORACE GREELEY   55

7 "I Was Not Born To Be Forced"
   HENRY DAVID THOREAU   67

8 The Branded Hand
   JONATHAN WALKER   79

9 "If the Women Mean To Wear the Pants"
   AMELIA JENKS BLOOMER   85

10 "The Minority Are Right!"
EUGENE DEBS   95

11 "I Believe That Men Will See the Truth"
WOODROW WILSON   107

12 First Female Doctor in the West
BETHENIA OWENS   121

13 "The Law Was Wrong, Not I"
MARGARET SANGER   131

14 "The Atomic Clock Ticks Faster"
J. ROBERT OPPENHEIMER   145

15 "My God, I Feel So Alone!"
J. WILLIAM FULBRIGHT   157

BIBLIOGRAPHY   179

INDEX   183

FOREWORD

You might suspect, from the title, that this is going to be a teenage angst-fest, a depressing saga of popular versus unpopular kids.

It's actually much more momentous: fifteen true stories of Americans in stark conflict with their times. They spoke their minds even when others strongly disagreed, and being "unpopular" was the least of their problems. These outlaws were tortured, pelted with rotten eggs and animal manure, branded with a hot iron, imprisoned, humiliated, run out of town, and more. From Roger Williams (fighting the good fight for religious freedom and the separation of church and state) to J. William Fulbright (who, in one of the most revelatory chapters, did everything in his power to make Americans more worldly and sophisticated), these were heroes for being on the right side of history even when it hurt.

This book is nothing less than a party in honor of one of our most cherished freedoms, the freedom of speech. First published in the tumultuous, protest-filled year of 1968, it was part of the America in the Making series.

I was lucky enough to know Jules Archer. While working as a senior editor at Harcourt I took on his *Winners and Losers: How Elections Work in America* (1984), which was a *School Library Journal* "Best Book" and a Notable Children's Trade Book in the Field of Social Studies. Then I worked with him on a title dear to my heart—*The Incredible Sixties: The Stormy Years that Changed America* (1986), another *SLJ* "Best Book."

I knew Jules Archer to be a passionate idealist, hugely concerned with inspiring young people to become informed citizens, anxious about righting society's wrongs and helping as much as possible. Unlike some other authors I won't name, Archer was always a total professional, dependable, and a pleasure to work with. Archer's reviews were always stellar, making him a go-to person for social studies nonfiction.

At one point I traveled from San Diego to meet Archer in Santa Cruz. In person he was courtly, kind, great company. All his life he remained politically active, while also roller-skating, playing chess, and writing away. He was perhaps the most prolific writer of nonfiction books for young people of his day.

This book is one for dipping into—and naturally I turned to the women first. Amelia Bloomer we know as justifiably famous for donning pants in 1851. Bloomers caught on—an early symbol for women's independence—despite the first wearers being harassed by mobs of males howling crude remarks. As with all his subjects, Archer gives us a full biographical portrait, explaining how Bloomer arrived at her unpopular stance on pants.

It was daring of him to include Margaret Sanger, still controversial (in some circles) after all these years. Starting in 1912, horrified at what the high birthrate did to women's health, Sanger dared to publish information on birth control. For trying to help women be more in control over their lives, she lost her husband, gained powerful enemies, and was imprisoned for obscenity. She never gave up, no matter the obstacles, and went on to found Planned Parenthood—she is a true American heroine.

Bethenia Owens was a new name to me. We know Elizabeth Blackwell as the first woman doctor in America, practicing in New York. But Owens, facing enormous, fascinating challenges, was for a time the only woman doctor in the entire West. Threatened with being tarred and feathered, she was instead run out of one town and forced to move to another.

The person most deserving of a book of her own is Anne Royall, one of Archer's quirkier choices. Known for publishing brutally honest opinions about religion, politicians, and everything else, she was America's first woman journalist. The punishments for her were harsh: once an enemy beat her so severely she couldn't walk for three years, and, in 1829, she was tried and found guilty of being a "Common Scold," barely escaping the humiliation of the ducking stool.

Archer's quirkiest choice is Joseph Palmer, a man who suffered mightily in 1830 Massachusetts because he dared to wear . . . a large bushy beard. (It was a time when smooth faces on men were de rigueur.) Also new to me was Jonathan Walker, one of the earliest abolitionists, who actively helped Florida slaves escape. In 1844, he was thrown in jail, chained, and branded with a hot iron—"SS" for "Slave Stealer—all described in nauseating detail.

Possibly the biggest hero in the book is heavy thinker Henry David Thoreau. The ultimate nonconformist, he's guided everyone from Gandhi to Dr. Martin Luther King Jr. to many protestors today. He didn't suffer for his beliefs as much as some others did, but he strikes a contemporary note that could make a good tattoo: "The fear of displeasing the world ought not in the least to influence my actions."

And there's much more. John Peter Zenger, who went a long way to uphold freedom of the press in America. Thomas Paine, the *Common Sense* guy who was one of the architects of the American Revolution. Horace Greeley, who not only said, "Go West, young man," but also advocated a plethora of causes unpopular enough to bring constant death threats. Eugene Debs, always on the side of the workers, not the 1 percent. Woodrow Wilson, for his promotion of the international peacekeeping organization that became the United Nations. J. Robert Oppenheimer, who created the atom bomb and was shunned for speaking out against its use.

The careful reader will learn a ton of American history here—slightly in the vein of contemporary historian Howard Zinn, including the outsiders, not skirting from controversy.

Archer enlivens his material with a brisk, newspaper-y style, contagious enthusiasm, and a wry sense of humor. He boils his intensive research down into accessible paragraphs that flow, cutting through complex material to render it clear.

By today's standards, the book could use more diversity. It also suffers the occasional blurring of fact and fiction—definitely untrendy today—like what his heroes were thinking and what is clearly invented dialogue.

But where is our Jules Archer now, urging young people to speak up and get involved, chronicling the deeds of Edward Snowden, Martin Luther King Jr., Harvey Milk, the Occupy movement, Cesar Chavez, Malala Yousafzai, and on and on?

The theme of the book is as timely as ever.

—Kathleen Krull

INTRODUCTION

People are often shocked whenever a clergyman declares, as many have done, that if Jesus of Nazareth were to walk our streets today and preach his "anti-Establishment" doctrines as he did in the days of the Romans, he would be crucified again. Not on a cross, perhaps, but he would probably be vilified as a Communist subversive and attacked by mobs. In some states he might also be thrown in jail for vagrancy, loitering, or causing disturbances.

How really tolerant of unpopular ideas have we learned to be today? The once despised cult of Christianity has, with the passage of time, become so respectable that it underlies our whole Western civilization. Yet many Christians today are just as intolerant of differences of opinion as the early Romans were toward the Christian protest movement.

We tend to forget, too, that the great government of the United States of America was once only a "treasonous" idea in the minds of a band of revolutionists who were highly unpopular with the vast majority of their fellow citizens in the mother country. Many of their fellow colonists also considered them unpatriotic traitors to the British crown.

A wit was once asked how history decided who was a traitor and who was a patriot. "That's simple," he replied. "A traitor is an unsuccessful revolutionist. A patriot is a successful one. Whether you get hung, or have a statue erected to you as a founding father, depends entirely on how the battle turns out. If England had crushed our uprising, our history books today would brand George Washington a treasonous scoundrel and hail Benedict Arnold as a noble hero!"

Thoughtful citizens do not jeer at or dismiss an idea simply because it is unpopular at the time it is advanced. They may decide against it after listening to its pleaders and weighing arguments on the other side. But it's intolerant and short-sighted to close one's mind to an idea or opinion simply because it's different from what most of us have been taught to believe.

One need only remember Galileo, who so incensed the Establishment of his day by his insistence that the earth revolved around the sun, and not the sun around the almighty earth, that he was tortured to force him to recant his "abominable heresy."

In the great play *Enemy of the People*, Henrik Ibsen makes the point that today's majority was once yesterday's hooted-at minority. It often takes a generation, Ibsen said, for a minority opinion that is sound to be fully understood, to prevail, and to become majority opinion.

This is not to say, obviously, that *every* minority opinion is destined to win out in the end. Most crusading Don Quixotes who tilt at windmills die away and are forgotten. But among them are *some* voices of protest—the truest, best, or most per-suasive—that steadily grow in the winds of change, and eventually win over the minds of their countrymen.

This book is about fifteen Americans, some famous, some obscure, who were persecuted in their time for their minority beliefs—the same beliefs that today have become accepted as part of our way of life. Their stories are reminders to all of us of the need to be tolerant and broad-minded, in the best tradition of the American Bill of Rights.

Only when we respect the voices of protest and give them a fair chance to be heard can we be certain we are not vilify-ing, persecuting, or crucifying those among us today who hold unpopular minority opinions. We will be glad of our tolerance tomorrow, because some of them, like the fifteen idealistic crusaders in this book, will eventually be proved right and the whole nation will benefit from their foresight.

THE UNPOPULAR ONES

FIFTEEN AMERICAN MEN AND WOMEN WHO STOOD UP FOR WHAT THEY BELIEVED IN

I

"Newe and Dangerous Opinions"

Roger Williams

The colonists of Salem flocked to town that chill morning of October 9, 1635, buzzing with excitement about the trial of thirty-two-year-old Roger Williams. The Massachusetts colony had had enough of the "bad penny" teacher and minister who stirred up trouble wherever he went. Either he would recant his seditious views, or the General Court sitting in Newton Church that morning would banish him out of the colony.

What else was to be done with a fanatic—person of quality though he was—who preached defiantly that "no one should be bound to maintain a worship against his own consent"? A fine world this would be, indeed, if everyone just worshiped according to his whim, instead of according to the law!

The colony of Massachusetts required every man to attend regular services at the Puritan Congregational Church and to pay for its support. What man in his right mind—or soul— would challenge the right of the government to enforce the Ten Commandments? Yet Williams dared protest against that, too. And he objected when decisions reached by preachers at "synod" meetings were enforced along with civil laws.

The Massachusetts authorities were opposed to Master Williams for yet another reason. He questioned their very right to the land they had colonized. The King had no power to grant it to them, Williams insisted, because it belonged to the American Indians. The Puritans' righteous colony, therefore, was flourishing on stolen ground! The outraged authorities dreaded that such insolence, reaching the King's ears, might anger him so that he would revoke their charter. Roger Williams simply had to be driven out of the colony as a dangerous, subversive influence.

The crowded church grew hushed as the defendant entered to face the grave charges against him. Fifty magistrates of the colony regarded him grimly from benches above the rostrum. His good-looking English features firm with conviction, he faced the magistrates resolutely. The Governor arose and in a bored voice droned out the charges against the defendant.

All too familiar with his alleged "crimes," Roger Williams let his thoughts drift back to the chain of events that had led him to this moment of judgment. He saw again the green valleys of Wales where he'd been born in 1603, son of a merchant tailor. He'd been rescued from the world of tradesmen by the interest of Sir Edward Coke, a lawyer who first employed him as a clerk, then put him through London's Charterhouse School and Cambridge University.

Falling under the influence of Calvinists intent upon reforming the rigid Anglican Church of England, he had become ordained as a minister in 1628. Chaplain to the Essex household of Sir William Masham, he'd met such leading Puritan reformers as Oliver Cromwell and Thomas Hooker. The Puritans, he felt, did not go far enough in their opposition to the Church of England. But he welcomed the opportunity to emigrate to their Massachusetts Bay colony, eager to taste the intoxicating atmosphere of religious freedom in the New World.

He arrived in Salem the morning of February 5, 1631, aboard the ship *Lyon,* which was carrying supplies to the colony. To his dismay, he discovered that the Puritans had established a new Congregational Church every bit as intolerant as the Church of

England they had fled from. Convinced that they alone knew the true will of God, they had made church membership a requirement for voting and holding land. Citizens were punished for failing to attend church regularly, obey the Ten Commandments, or pay taxes to support the established church.

Serving briefly as a church teacher, Williams found the colony's religious regimentation too oppressive and left for the Plymouth colony. Here the break with the dour spirit of the Church of England was sharper. But he ran into a buzz saw of public opinion when he insisted that the colony ought to pay the Indians for the land they had confiscated, obtaining a just title.

Indignant Plymouth settlers drove him back to Salem in 1633. For two years he was barely tolerated as a pastor, as he continued to voice his unpopular protests. Church and state must be entirely separate, he insisted stubbornly. It was folly to compel men to attend church against their will. The government must calmly tolerate all religious dissenters from the established Congregational Church and respect their rights to worship as they pleased as long as they behaved well.

Colony leaders warned him to hold his tongue. Williams refused to listen. Their patience exhausted, they arraigned him for spreading "newe and dangerous opinions, against the authoritie of magistrates."

Now the Governor, winding up his reading of the charges, asked Roger Williams if he was ready to answer them. If not, the General Court would, "in all fairness," give him a month's delay to prepare his defense, or he could, upon reflection, recant.

Williams smiled bitterly. The General Court was, as well as his judge and jury, the colony's legislature. By the act of bringing him to trial, his accusers, changing hats to sit in judgment, had made the Court's verdict inevitable.

But perhaps his words could stir the people of the colony into demanding true justice and freedom from their leaders.

"I am ready to answer now," he replied calmly.

The Court named as its prosecutor Thomas Hooker—the same Puritan whom Williams had met at Essex.

Williams's cry for "religious liberty," Hooker charged, was in effect a betrayal of the principles that had united all Puritans when they risked the American wilderness to worship together in their own church. Worse, Williams was going against the will of God in challenging the right of religious leaders to rule the people. Was it for the people to rule religious leaders? That was as absurd as passengers refusing to obey a ship's officers and telling the captain and his men how to sail the ship!

Roger Williams replied that every man was captain of his own soul. The manner in which he worshiped was solely between himself and his God. There were many roads to heaven, and no man was wise enough to know the best. It was not possible for any community to be made up entirely of true believers, therefore it was unjust for the majority to force their own religious creeds upon the minority.

Furthermore, Williams challenged, no government had the right to say to a man that he could not enjoy the full privileges of a citizen unless he worshiped as he was told. Magistrates must not be masters of the people, but their servants. If his crime was that he believed in freedom of conscience, why, then yes, he was indeed guilty!

A grim-faced Governor rose to pronounce the colony's sentence of banishment: "Mr. Williams shall depart out of this jurisdiction within six weeks." He was, moreover, not to preach his doctrines during this grace period.

But Roger Williams refused to be silenced. Continuing to speak out in the weeks that followed, he so infuriated the government in Boston that they dispatched police to Salem with the intention of seizing him and putting him on a ship for England. A sympathizer raced ahead of the police, warning the rebel to flee instantly.

The early darkening of the vivid blue sky warned of the approaching winter, but Williams did not hesitate. He would find another place on American soil to establish a new colony for free men—men who would be *truly* free to worship as they pleased and to govern themselves. He knew that he was not alone in holding sacred freedom of conscience. Others would join him in exile when he had found a safe refuge.

He fled southwest into the wilderness, alone and on foot, hopefully seeking the Indian village of Sowans at the head of Narragansett Bay. During four hungry, freezing days of wandering, he wondered anxiously whether Chief Massasoit would receive him as a friend of the Indian people. Or would he be regarded as just another white Puritan who had invaded their country, taken their land, and sought to convert them to a Christianity that considered them savages?

He found Sowans. To his great relief, Massasoit knew of his fight on behalf of the Indians and considered him a blood brother. Fed and sheltered in Massasoit's own wigwam, Williams was respected as a sachem, or chief of high rank. The Narragansetts were impressed that he had been interested enough in Indian culture to study their language. They helped him improve his knowledge of it during his stay with them over the winter. His health suffered badly from exposure, but Massasoit's medicine men did what they could to alleviate his suffering.

While he was at Sowans an angry quarrel broke out between Massasoit and another chief, Canonicus. Both tribes prepared for war. But Williams dared intervene between them with appeals for peace, pointing out how senseless it was for hundreds of Indians to die over a dispute that could be settled more satisfactorily by conciliation. Their respect for him was so great that both chiefs agreed to a peace powwow.

It was successful. The impressed and grateful Canonicus offered Roger Williams a gift of gratitude—land for his colony. Delighted, the exile sent word to five friends in Salem. They lost no time in joining him in his new cabin on the Seekonk River.

But they brought word that the land there would not do; the Massachusetts colony had claimed it.

So they paddled down the Seekonk in Indian canoes until they reached Narragansett Bay and found land with a spring of sweet water. Roger Williams named their settlement Providence because he felt that the beautiful area they had discovered had been "God's merciful Providence to us in our distress." To legalize their claim, he insisted upon paying the Indians for this land. Then in 1636 he and his followers set to work building homes in a new outpost of freedom.

They built a Baptist church, but Williams proclaimed complete tolerance in the settlement for Protestants, Catholics, Jews, and atheists. In 1639 he described himself as a Seeker—one who adhered to basic Christianity but refused to recognize any creed as being the official road to salvation.

He made certain that the government of Providence was freely elected by the vote of all citizens, and that it limited itself to civil affairs only: "None bee accounted a Delinquent for Doctrine." Elected representatives were made responsible to the colonists—government by consent of the governed.

These revolutionary ideas attracted thousands of settlers eager to worship as they pleased and to control their own destinies. Leaders of the Massachusetts colony that had banished Roger Williams were indignant. What wild nonsense to tell people that they had the right not only to create their own government, but also to limit its powers or change it as they pleased! Where every head of a family was given an *equal* voice in that government!

To stop the spread of Williams's seditious doctrines, the authorities in Boston severely punished dissenters. On November 8, 1637, they tried Anne Hutchinson and thirty followers for heresy, and banished them. Another group led by William Coddington left Boston voluntarily. Both showed up at Providence and asked Roger Williams to help them buy land from the Indians for their own colonies. He gladly assisted them in founding two more Rhode Island colonies, Portsmouth and Newport.

That same year, 1638, Williams had a tempting opportunity for revenge against the Puritans who had driven him into the wilderness. The Narragansetts were being stirred up by the Pequots to massacre Bostonians while the Pequots attacked Connecticut settlers. Warned by Indian friends, Williams quickly used his influence to persuade the Narragansetts not to go on the warpath. The humanity of the man the Massachusetts colonists had persecuted as a heretic was responsible for saving thousands of their lives.

Williams's contacts with the Indians, always for the purpose of fostering peaceful relations between white and red men, as well as between tribe and tribe, led him to conclude that the Puritans were wrong in their belief that the red men needed conversion. "My God would not be displeased," he told Indian chiefs, "because your people worship him differently than we Christians do. It would be wrong to make Indians follow the white man's forms of worship. Who is to say which God finds more pleasing?" In the Rhode Island colony he discouraged all attempts to convert Indians to Christianity.

Watching other colonies springing up in Connecticut, Williams decided to go to England to secure an official charter from Parliament to protect Rhode Islanders from encroachment. In 1643 Parliament had become the new power in England, as Cromwell led its Roundhead armies against King Charles I. Williams was enthusiastically welcomed both by Cromwell and poet John Milton. He supported the Reformation movement with a widely read pamphlet called *The Bloudy Tenent* [Bloody Tenet] *of Persecution for Cause of Conscience*.

"God requireth not a uniformity of religion to be enacted and enforced in any civil state," he wrote in 1644, "which enforced uniformity (sooner or later) is the occasion of civil war, ravishing of conscience, persecution of Jesus Christ in his servants,

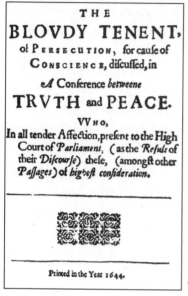

THE
BLOVDY TENENT,
of Persecution, for caufe of
Conscience, difcuffed, in

A Conference *betweene*
TRVTH and **PEACE.**

VV ho,
In all tender Affection, prefent to the High
Court of *Parliament,* (asthe *Refult* of
their *Difcourfe*) thefe, (amongft other
Paffages) of *higheft confideration.*

Printed in the Year 1644.

The title page of *The Bloudy Tenent.*

and of the hypocrisy and destruction of millions of souls." He pointed out that the only alternative to the senseless slaughter of innocent people who refused to worship as they were told was a free society in which all agreed to tolerate each other's differences—a government that would preserve peace, protect individual rights, and promote the good of all.

The pamphlet would have cost him his head except for the turmoil of the civil war between King and Parliament. Instead, Parliament granted him a charter uniting the four colonies of Rhode Island into a province, and conceded them full powers of self-government. His triumphant return to America with the charter infuriated the Massachusetts Bay General Court into issuing an edict banishing all Baptists from their midst. Let all dissenters join the madman Roger Williams in his colonies ruled by the Devil!

The apostle of dissent, meanwhile, found dissent breaking out against the new charter. William Coddington led the opposition to unifying Rhode Island's four colonies under a single government. It took three years of squabbling before they united under "a government held by the free and voluntarie consent of all, or the greater parte of the free inhabitants." All were guaranteed freedom of conscience and separation of church and state. It was the first great American experiment in democracy and religious toleration.

Roger Williams was elected president of the new colony for three consecutive terms. Characteristically, when Jewish immigrants were barred from all the other colonies, it was he who flung open the ports of Rhode Island to them. The first synagogue in America appeared in Newport in 1658.

When the Quakers were hung, flogged and jailed, and driven out of every New England colony, they too found refuge in Rhode Island. Williams also saw to it that, on all ships the colony controlled bringing immigrants to the New World, "none of the Papists, Protestants, Jews or Turks be forced to come to the ship's prayer or worship nor compelled from their own particular prayer or worship, if they practise any."

His incendiary views not only outraged other New England colonies, but also worried the British Parliament. While opposing the tyranny of King Charles I, they feared that Williams's bold ideas were making the British masses *too* revolutionary. So all copies of his *Bloudy Tenent* were ordered seized and burned. In an ironic turn of the tables, it was the next King, Charles II, who gave Williams's colony England's blessings with a royal charter in 1663.

That recognition, won because of the King's need of revenue, made Rhode Island a little republic within the British Empire—the freest community on earth of its time. It remained so through the Revolution over a hundred years later.

Roger Williams died in 1683. The unpopular gadfly of the Massachusetts colony, the outlaw, the madman, the heretic, the subversive, the minority of one—he proved by his vision, courage, and idealism that he had been right and the whole government of Massachusetts had been wrong. He had faced persecution, banishment, and suffering for his convictions.

But the United States of America was built on the foundation *he* laid, not on that of the powerful majority he challenged. Our government today has erected two monuments to Roger Williams that he would have cherished.

The first is the Preamble to the Constitution: "We the people of the United States, in Order to form a more perfect Union, establish Justice, insure domestic Tranquility, provide for the common defense, promote the general Welfare, and secure the Blessings of Liberty to ourselves and our Posterity, do ordain and establish this Constitution for the United States of America."

The second is the First Amendment of the Bill of Rights: "Congress shall make no law respecting an establishment of religion, or prohibiting the free exercise thereof."

Roger Williams was not vindicated in *all* the ideals he cherished. But perhaps someday there may be a third monument to him in a Constitutional amendment that says: "Congress shall reimburse the descendants of all Indian tribes for the lands taken from their forefathers without fair payment."

2

Morning Star of Liberty

John Peten Zenger

An imperious knock of the brass clapper at the front door of his house on Broad Street caught John Peter Zenger stirring a pitcher of flip with a red-hot poker. Annoyed at this interruption of his Sunday afternoon relaxation, he buttoned his doublet and straightened his black broadcloth knee breeches as he went to the door.

Opening it, he found the doorway filled by the massive bulk of John Symes. The Sheriff of New York held a rolled scroll in his hand like a majestic scepter.

"Citizen John Peter Zenger?"

"What new harassment now?" Zenger sighed. His German accent made his consonants guttural; he had been a naturalized citizen for only twelve years. "Is it not enough for Governor Cosby to seize copies of my newspaper and order them burned by the hangman? What more is in store for me, Sheriff?"

Sheriff Symes unrolled the scroll with a flourish.

"It is ordered that the Sheriff for the City of New York do forthwith take and apprehend John Peter Zenger, for printing and publishing several Seditious libels dispersed throughout his Newspaper entitled *The New York Weekly Journal,* containing the freshest Advices, foreign and domestic; as having in them many Things, tending to raise Factions and Tumults, among the People of this Province, inflaming their Minds with Contempt of His Majesty's Government, and greatly disturbing the Peace thereof, and upon his taking the said John Peter Zenger, to commit him to the Prison or common Gaol of said City and County. By order of the King's Council under warrant of His Excellency Governor William Cosby."

Zenger blinked incredulously. "But the Council has no power to order my arrest! And they have no right to jail me on a mere opinion—unsupported by any evidence!"

"My orders are to arrest you at once, Citizen Zenger."

"You can't! There must be a trial first. And you must allow me to seek counsel. Let me write a letter at least—"

Symes stiffened. "At *once,* Citizen Zenger!"

So on November 17, 1734, John Peter Zenger, who had imagined himself safe from the tyranny of a European monarchy in the New World, found himself flung into a dark dungeon. Day after day his demand to seek counsel was denied, as was the use of pen, ink, and paper. On the Monday following his arrest. New Yorkers looked for the new issue of his *Weekly Journal.* They were baffled by its failure to appear.

Where was Zenger?

Born somewhere in Germany in 1697, he had immigrated to the Colonies with his family when he was thirteen. His father had died on the arduous Atlantic crossing. Arriving in New York, the stunned young immigrant won refuge as an apprentice of the Quaker printer-publisher William Bradford.

Bradford had left Philadelphia after a newspaper he had edited there had been suppressed for "seditious libel" in 1691. Establishing the first press in the New York colony, he taught Zenger not only the art of printing but also the duty of publishers to give free voice to public discontent.

In 1725, for a brief while, Zenger became Bradford's junior partner in the colony's first newspaper, the *New York Gazette.* But a year later he left to establish his own print shop, where he published a few political tracts, Dutch religious books, and

Vanema's Arithmetica, the first book on arithmetic printed in the colony. Eking out only a meager living, he was too poor to start a newspaper of his own until a political crisis in November 1733 made it possible.

When Dutch-settled New Amsterdam had fallen to the British in 1664, becoming New York, the colonists had found themselves oppressed by a despotism that allowed a Governor to tax them for his personal benefit as well as for the English crown. He also had the power to veto any act of the people's Assembly, as well as to dissolve it, whenever he pleased.

One of the worst of the English governors was William Cosby, whose brief rule from 1732 to 1736 was so arbitrary that it almost provoked New Yorkers to revolution. He was a British Army colonel of limited education and intelligence—personally greedy, arrogant, pompous, hot-tempered, and contemptuous of conciliation. His first act was to reject a gift of 750 pounds voted by the Assembly to conciliate him, insisting that it must be raised to 1000 pounds.

Cosby then demanded that Rip Van Dam, Dutch senior councilor of the King's Council, give him half the salary and fees paid Van Dam for serving as temporary Governor until the arrival of Cosby. Van Dam indignantly refused. Furious, Cosby set up the colony's Supreme Court as a special court of equity to rule against Van Dam. When Chief Justice Lewis Morris sought to be impartial, Cosby threw him out of office.

Morris thereupon became a candidate in the colony election of 1733. But Cosby had already secretly sold the office he sought to its incumbent occupant for a hundred pistoles. When New York's Quakers flocked to the polls to vote for Morris, Cosby had them disqualified for refusing to swear an election oath, despite their offer to "affirm" instead. (Quakers opposed oath-taking as creating a double standard of truth; they held one should *always* be truthful, under oath or not.) This was the last straw. New Yorkers were fed up with a corrupt Governor who also refused land grants to settlers unless they agreed to make over a third of their grants to him personally.

"We are Tenants at Will to Governors," Van Dam protested, "and exposed to be fleeced by them from Time to Time at their Pleasure." The colony divided into two political parties—the Royal Court Party, headed by Cosby, and the Popular Party, whose voice was the people's Assembly.

Van Dam, Morris, and other leaders of the Popular Party felt the need of a newspaper to expose Cosby publicly and arouse popular opinion against him. Bradford's *Gazette* was a captive to Cosby's control and censorship. So they approached Peter Zenger and offered to finance a paper for him if he would agree to print the truth about the Governor.

On November 5, 1733, the first issue of *The New York Weekly Journal* created a sensation with charges against Cosby written largely by Lewis Morris and other intellectuals of the Popular Party. The paper was such an instant success that Zenger was forced to increase his print run with each succeeding issue. The *Journal* scourged the Governor for denying Van Dam a trial by jury. Anyone who subverted the law in this manner, it declared defiantly, "is an enemy and traytor to his country." Royalists were outraged.

Rumors swept through the New York colony that Cosby, in retaliation, would shut down the *Journal.* On November 12, 1733, Zenger's paper warned, "The Liberty of the Press is a Subject of the greatest Importance, and in which every Individual is as much concerned as he is in any other Part of Liberty." One week later it warned even more grimly, "No nation ancient or modern ever lost the Liberty of freely speaking, writing, or publishing their Sentiments, but forthwith lost their Liberty in general and became Slaves."

Popular opinion, inflamed by Zenger's crusading paper, swung solidly behind the Popular Party. When they won a sweeping victory in an Aldermanic election, New Yorkers staged a great celebration. Jubilant speeches were delivered in front of torchlit houses, and New Yorkers sang victory songs from leaflets Zenger had printed for the occasion:

Come on, brave boys, let us be brave for liberty and law,
Boldly despise the haughty Knave that would keep us in awe. . . .
Our Country's Rights we will defend, like brave and honest men,
We voted right and there's an end, and men, we'll so do again. . . .
Tho' great men do assert no flaw is in them, they shall fall,
And be condemned by every man that's fond of liberty!

Frightened by the winds of revolution, Governor Cosby hastily prepared two proclamations. The first offered a reward of twenty pounds for the apprehension of the author of "two Printed Scandalous Songs or Ballads, highly defaming the Administration of His Majesty's Government in this Province, tending greatly to inflame the Minds of His Majesty's Good Subjects, and to disturb the Public Peace."

The second proclamation offered fifty pounds for the apprehension of the author of "divers Scandalous, Virulent, False and Seditious Reflections" printed in Zenger's weekly *Journal.* The King's Council then demanded that the Assembly issue these proclamations and also condemn four issues of Zenger's paper, which were to be delivered into the hands of the common hangman to be publicly burned as seditious.

The people's Assembly defiantly refused. Enraged, Cosby issued the proclamations himself on November 6, 1734.

Sheriff John Symes burned the offending issues of the *Journal* in a public square. Then eleven days later John Peter Zenger found himself arrested and thrown into jail.

When the Popular Party discovered what had happened, they rushed a lawyer to his assistance with a writ of habeas corpus to procure his freedom until a date of trial. But after Zenger revealed that he did not have forty pounds above his debts, clothes, and printing press, bail was set at an exorbitant four hundred pounds to keep him in prison. That, Cosby hoped, would force the *Journal* to suspend publication.

Zenger was compelled to languish in prison until the following August—nine months. But the Popular Party thwarted Cosby's plot when its lawyers forced court permission for Zenger to speak to his wife regularly through "the Hole of the Door of the Prison." In this way Zenger defiantly continued to publish the *Journal* from his cell.

When Zenger's lawyers challenged the legality of the proceedings against him, Cosby had them disbarred for their temerity. "You thought to have gained a great Deal of Applause and Popularity by opposing this Court," the Chief Justice ruled, "but you have brought it to that Point that either We must go from the Bench or you from the Barr."

Prevented from defending Zenger themselves, his lawyers rushed to Philadelphia to enlist the services of the celebrated, eighty-year-old Andrew Hamilton. The case came to trial on August 4, 1735, at the City Hall on the corner of Nassau and Wall Streets. The courtroom was jammed with excited New Yorkers. If Zenger were found guilty, they felt, any hope of getting rid of Governor Cosby would be lost. But if he were found innocent, Cosby's tyranny would stand publicly exposed by the law of the colony.

Other colonies were also following the trial closely. No other event had ever dealt so directly with the rights of colonists under British sovereignty.

The judges, in their robes and elaborate wigs, took their places on the bench. Ten men filled the jury box. Only then did Governor Cosby discover, to his dismay, that the Popular Party had secured the brilliant Andrew Hamilton to defend Zenger. In panic he sent secret word to the Bench to find a pretext for excluding Hamilton from the case. But the judges, fearful of provoking a riot, did not dare.

The Sheriff burned the offending issues of the *Journal* in a public square.

Attorney General John Chambers proposed to prove that Zenger was guilty of printing and publishing "a false, scandalous and seditious Libel" of His Excellency, the Governor. He cited all the accusations against Cosby that Zenger had published in the *Journal*. Hamilton admitted that Zenger had, indeed, printed all these accusations. But how did that make him guilty of the crime of libel? The accusations were true, Hamilton asserted— and he intended to prove it!

"Supposing they were true," Chambers argued frantically. "The Law says that they are not the less libellous for that! Nay, indeed the Law says their being true is an *aggravation* of the crime!" He quoted the Bible: "Thou shalt not speak evil of the Ruler of the People." Zenger, Chambers insisted, had violated the law of both God and man by creating a scandal about the Governor, the "King's immediate representative." He must be punished for stirring sedition and discontent!

Nonsense, rebutted Hamilton. The charge against Zenger accused him of publishing *false* libel, did it not? "This word *false* must have some Meaning, or how came it there? . . . No, the Falsehood makes the Scandal, and both make the Libel. . . . *If* he can prove the Facts charged upon us to be *false*, I'll own them to be *scandalous, seditious and a libel!*"

Startled, the Court refused to let him pursue this line of defense. Hamilton sarcastically asked the judges how it could be possible "that Truth is a greater Sin Than Falsehood?" Warned he must say no more about this, he told the jury pointedly, "The suppressing of Evidence ought always to be taken for the strongest evidence—and I hope it will have weight with you!"

The Chief Justice angrily instructed the jury, "You may only decide whether Zenger printed and published those Papers, and leave it to the Court to judge whether they are libellous." He reminded them sternly, "It is very necessary for all Governments that the People should have a good Opinion of it." Criticism of an administration had to be looked upon as a criminal act—"and no Government can be safe without it be punished!"

The jury took only minutes to deliberate. When they returned, they announced a unanimous verdict—"*Not* guilty!"

The City Hall exploded with roars of delight and cheers.

Chagrined, the Court set John Peter Zenger free.

Enthusiastic admirers gave a dinner in Hamilton's honor at the Black Horse Tavern. When he sailed for Philadelphia, ships in the harbor fired a salute to his brilliant defense of freedom in the Colonies. The Common Council of New York sent him a gold box engraved with the city's coat of arms. Newspapers carried glowing accounts of his victory to Americans everywhere—and to London.

The implications of the Zenger case were far-reaching.

A jury had dared defy the Crown-controlled Court that had ordered it to condemn published criticism of the government, whether it was true or not. By its vote of "Not guilty," the jury had clearly held that *truthful* criticism of a corrupt government was *not* libelous. Its verdict had also asserted the right of colonial justice to prevail over Royal edict. The winds of independence were stirring.

Governor Cosby died in March 1736, utterly discredited, little mourned. Upon his death a more intelligent new Governor, George Clarke, appointed John Peter Zenger the colony's public printer. A year later Zenger was also appointed public printer for New Jersey. He continued printing the *Journal,* independently and fearlessly, until his death on July 28, 1746, at the age of forty-nine. The paper continued under his wife, then his son John, for another five years.

The Zenger case sounded the death knell for government censorship of the press through judges. No longer could they allot to themselves the right to decide when libel had been committed. After Zenger, the jury's right to make that decision instead protected freedom of the press in America. Significantly, fifty-six years later the English Parliament itself admitted the colonists had been right by giving British juries the same right.

Following Zenger's victory, Americans vigorously exercised their right to criticize the conduct of Crown-appointed officials. An unchained press united them in the struggle against British oppression. "The trial of Zenger in 1735," said Governor Morris, "was the germ of American freedom, the morning star of that liberty which subsequently revolutionized America."

John Peter Zenger was buried in New York's Trinity Churchyard, but his monument—like Roger Williams's—was erected in the Constitution of the United States: the First Amendment, guaranteeing Americans a free press in which they have the right to criticize the government whenever they wish.

3

"Whether it Be Popular or Unpopular"

Thomas Paine

As he lay dying in a shabby rented house in old Greenwich Village, enraged Americans besieged him to demand that he repent his blasphemies before he went to Hell. Others flocked to gawk at the "loathesome reptile" and "lying, drunken, brutal infidel," as the Federalist press described him.

When he died, the usually tolerant Quakers refused to bury him in a Quaker cemetery. Yet Thomas Paine was as much the father of his country as George Washington.

He was born in England at Thetford, Norfolk, son of a Quaker corsetmaker, on January 29, 1737. The first thirty-six years of his life were a record of hardship and failure. He spent two years at sea on the crew of a privateer; was fired as a tax collector for being too softhearted; fled into hiding to escape debtors' prison when a tobacconist's shop that he opened failed. Given a second chance as a tax collector, he was fired again for writing the grievances of his fellow excisemen in a petition to Parliament. To add to his troubles, a first wife died in childbirth; a second wife left him.

Despairing of ever rising out of this wretched life as long as he remained in England, Paine decided to leave for the New World. He called upon the London agent for the colony of Pennsylvania,

Benjamin Franklin, with whom he had been exchanging letters about the latter's experiments with electricity. Franklin saw a hungry-looking man with a long, thin nose, high forehead, sensitive mouth, and large eyes like fiery coals. Impressed with Paine's intellect, Franklin generously helped pay his passage to Philadelphia.

"The bearer, Mr. Thomas Paine, is very well recommended to me as an ingenious, worthy young man," Franklin wrote with greater kindness than veracity in a letter of introduction to his son-in-law. Soon after Paine's arrival in America on November 30, 1774, the letter won him a job as editor of the monthly *Pennsylvania Magazine*. Despite his brief schooling, Paine had studied great writers like Swift, Addison, and Dr. Johnson. They had stimulated him to think profoundly and originally, and to express his thoughts with clarity and fire.

His editorship was the first success of his life. In less than two years his views were the talk of the Colonies. Many were scandalized, many delighted, by his demands for better treatment of wives, rights for labor, political and economic freedom, and limitation of Royal power.

Acting as a gadfly to American discontent with King George III, Paine was supremely indifferent to his tiny salary and one cramped room. He worked persistently toward a goal that fired him with zeal—independence for America. But George Washington was warning colonists that independence was not desired "by any thinking man in all North America." Franklin had been sent to London not to threaten, but to plead for tax relief for the Colonies.

In April 1775, however, British forces marched through the countryside outside Boston to intimidate colonials. The Battle of Lexington that resulted was "the shot heard 'round the world." Yet even as civil war broke out, delegates to the Philadelphia Continental Congress met only as "reluctant rebels," wanting only a greater measure of self-government.

Conservatives had no wish to create a revolution, as they dreaded the unruly forces this would release in the Colonies. Merchants depended heavily upon English trade privileges. But colonial outrage exploded when England hired foreign mercenaries to fight Englishmen and British agents provoked Indian attacks on frontier settlements.

Paine, boldest of the firebrands, called for revolution. This was too much for the conservative publisher of the *Pennsylvania Magazine,* who fired him. Undaunted, Paine plunged into the writing of a pamphlet he called *Common Sense.*

A declaration of independence, he insisted, was the only possible solution. He ridiculed monarchy: "In England a king hath little more to do than to make war and give away places. . . . A pretty business indeed for a man to be allowed eight hundred thousand sterling a year for, and worshipped into the bargain!" It was absurd, he pointed out, for "a Continent to be perpetually governed by an island."

And how could Americans pretend to be loyal to the Crown while fighting the King's troops on American soil? If they broke with England now, France would give them the foreign aid they needed to win their freedom. He urged colonists to rethink their habit of bowing to the Crown. "We have it in our power," he cried, "to begin the world over again!"

He trudged around Philadelphia until he found a printer who dared print *Common Sense*—for half the profits. The threadbare Paine not only agreed, but turned his half over to the cause of revolution. Published on January 10, 1776, at two shillings a copy, it caused an immediate sensation.

Within three months 120,000 copies were sold. It was read and eagerly discussed by cobblers in their shops, bakers by their ovens, teachers in their schools. Illiterates gathered in groups to hear it read aloud. By April, Washington was writing, "I find *Common Sense* is working a powerful change . . . in the minds of many men." John Adams found it hardening colonial sentiment for independence.

Tribute to the power of *Common Sense* even came from England, where British historian William Gordon wrote, "It has produced the most astonishing effects, and been received with vast applause, read by almost every American. . . . It has satisfied multitudes that it is in their true interest immediately to cut the Gordian knot by which the American colonies have been bound to Great Britain."

Outraged American Loyalists sought to dampen the fiery impact of *Common Sense* by maligning its author. Aristocrats like Governor Morris called Paine a drunkard, an unscrupulous adventurer from England, a low fellow who dressed filthily and mingled with the lowest trash of the taverns.

The charges were widely believed, but they did not deter Thomas Jefferson from befriending Paine and consulting him about a document of his own he had been asked to write. Many of Paine's ideas found their way into that document—the Declaration of Independence, adopted by the Continental Congress on July 4, 1776. Three weeks later Paine laid down his pen and joined the Pennsylvania volunteers, who were part of Washington's army fighting in New York.

He was made an aide-de-camp to General Nathaniel Greene. As they fell back in the harrowing retreat across the Jerseys, Paine watched in dismay as tattered, starved, and freezing American troops grew discouraged and began to desert.

To give fresh heart to the threadbare cause of independence, he wrote a series of tracts called *The Crisis*. Appearing in the middle of December 1776, *Crisis I* declared, "These are the times that try men's souls. The summer soldier and the sunshine patriot will, in this crisis, shrink from the service of his country; but he that stands it NOW, deserves the love and thanks of man and woman. . . . Tyranny, like hell, is not easily conquered; yet we have this consolation with us, that the harder the conflict, the more glorious the triumph."

Copies arrived two days before Christmas—one week after Washington's ragged army had been driven across the Delaware.

At dusk Washington lined his men up along the river in small groups, and *Crisis I* was read aloud to them by their sergeants and officers. Their chilled bodies caught fire with the burning eloquence of Paine's words. Pouring into the boats that took them back across the Delaware in darkness, they fell upon the unsuspecting British at Trenton. The badly needed victory raised American morale everywhere.

Paine's services to the Revolution were beyond value. Fighting beside Washington in the Battle of Germantown, he shared the frozen encampment at Valley Forge; slipped under British guns as liaison between American forts; raised money and supplies for the army; turned out more *Crisis* propaganda tracts to inspire disheartened Americans.

Crisis II warned General Howe that the Americans would never give up. "The United States of America," Paine wrote, "will sound as pompously in the world or in history as the Kingdom of Great Britain." It was the first time anyone had suggested a name for the new nation being born in revolution. Americans loved the majestic ring of it and adopted it.

Every new American crisis brought a new *Crisis* tract from Paine's stirring pen, buoying hopes in the darkest hours. As early as 1777 recognition of his services came with an appointment as Secretary to the Committee for Foreign Affairs of the Continental Congress. But in this post his patriotism provoked an uproar in the Silas Deane affair.

Deane, an American agent bringing back French funds secretly provided by King Louis XVI, kept a fat commission for himself. Paine denounced him publicly as a profiteering scoundrel. This denunciation revealed to the British that the French King had intended the funds as an outright gift. The British angrily protested to the embarrassed French government. Deane's influential rich friends in Congress forced Paine out of his post.

Denied another government job, Paine began to feel pinched for money. His clothes grew shabby, his quarters shabbier. Once some of Deane's rich friends attacked him on the street, throwing him into a filthy gutter. Philadelphians who saw him stagger home spread additional tales of his drunkenness and squalid personal habits. But finally, in 1779, he was made clerk of the Pennsylvania Assembly.

When the war came to a close in 1783, Paine wrote in *Crisis XIII,* last of the series, "The times that tried men's souls are over—and the greatest and completest revolution the world ever knew, gloriously and happily accomplished."

But his own fortunes were now far less glorious. While other men had prospered on war profits, Congress had paid him only eight hundred dollars a year to write the *Crisis* tracts. And he had spent much of his own savings on the Revolution. Only pressure by General Washington led the state of New York to award him a New Rochelle farm, the Pennsylvania Assembly to make him a gift of five hundred pounds, and Congress to give him a three-thousand-dollar grant. They were small rewards for the one American, more than any other, who had inspired the Revolution, sustained it when it faltered, and urged it on to final victory.

It was Paine, too, who first urged that a Constitutional Convention be called in Philadelphia. But when he was passed over as a delegate, he left for Europe in 1787 to seek scientific endorsement for scale models of a pierless steel bridge he had invented.

He was in England two years later when the French Revolution began. Paine was thrilled. Now France was following America's example. He could not help replying when England's Edmund Burke attacked the French republicans in a tract, *Reflections on the Revolution in France.* In March 1791 Paine's rebuttal, *The Rights of Man,* angered his British hosts.

"Monarchy would not have continued so many ages in the world," he charged, "had it not been for the abuses it protects. It is the master fraud, which shelters all others." Men had the right to choose republicanism, he insisted, and not to be forced to submit to titled aristocrats born to power. Why did Burke shed tears over the plight of Marie Antoinette and King Louis—but none for the victims of their despotism?

On signal from England's outraged Prime Minister, William Pitt, the British press sought to discredit Paine by reviving the old rumors about his drunkenness and unreliability. Burke wrote a reply to Paine, defending England's royalist tradition and urging criminal prosecution for the American's insolence to the Crown. Enjoying the fight, Paine published Part II of *The Rights of Man* in February 1792.

He pointed out that all the money England had spent for wars, royalty, and political graft could instead have produced a paradise for the English people. "The trade of governing has always been monopolized by the most ignorant and the most rascally individuals of mankind," he charged—and monarchists were the worst. All England gasped at Paine's bold hint: "Never did so great an opportunity offer itself to England, and to all Europe, as is produced by the two revolutions of America and France. . . ."

Infuriated, Pitt promptly arrested Paine's printer and seized all copies of Part II. Charges of sedition were filed against the American firebrand. Mobs were set to burning his books publicly, hanging him in effigy, painting his name on their shoe soles so they could step on him, setting fire to the homes of any seen with him. There was general indignation at his violation of British hospitality, at the role he had played in the American Revolution, at his mockery of the Crown. Cries for his execution grew louder.

He finally fled to France only minutes ahead of the police sent to arrest him. Republican France gave him a hero's welcome. The National Convention in Paris rose to its feet in a thunderous ovation when he entered the chamber. Made an honorary citizen, he was elected a revolutionary delegate to the new First

TOM PAINE'S *Nightly Pest*

This British anti-Paine cartoon that appeared in 1792 shows Tom Paine in poverty, covered by his worn coat, while a rat on the table, his head in a trap, implies Paine's predicament. The imp of sedition (the "Nightly Pesf") is flying out the window.

Republic. He aligned himself with the idealistic Girondists, many of whom were his personal friends, rather than with the bloodthirsty Jacobins.

In January 1793 he pleaded with the Convention to spare the life of King Louis because of the aid the monarch had given to the American Revolution. But a majority of one vote out of 721 sent Louis to the guillotine. When the Terror swept the Girondists out of the Convention, Paine was seized, stripped of his honorary citizenship, and flung into prison.

He wrote several letters of appeal to President George Washington, who neither answered them nor came to his rescue. One principal reason was publication of his latest book, *The Age of Reason,* which appeared in America early in 1794.

A devastating attack on organized religion, it began, "I believe in one God, and no more; and I hope for happiness beyond this life." His position was not atheistic but deistic—belief in a God who created the world but did not intervene in its affairs or pass biblical miracles. "I do not believe in the creed professed by the Jewish church, by the Roman church, by the Greek church, by the Turkish church, by the Protestant church, nor by any church that I know of. My own mind is my own church."

He condemned formal churches as tools of the state, sharing power and profit as a reward for keeping the masses subdued. Scoffing at the concept of a vengeful God who visited the sins of the father upon innocent children, he declared, "Belief in a cruel God makes a cruel man." He reaffirmed his belief in the equality of man—"and I believe that religious duties consist in doing justice, loving mercy, and endeavoring to make our fellow-creatures happy."

Nothing Paine had ever written created so great a furor. He had meant it as a reproach to the European system of state-supported religions, with America the inspiring example of a government that separated church and state. But it was in America that the greatest outcry rose against him as a heretic, anti-Christ, blasphemer, atheist.

The press vilified him; the clergy called down God's punishment on his head; his political enemies fought any move to rescue him from prison in France. His religious dissent was used to discredit his political beliefs about liberalism, democracy, free speech, open debate, a strong centralized union, equal rights, and tolerance for all. If he had been a hero of the Revolution, now no American was more unpopular.

On November 6, 1794, following the fall of Robespierre, he was finally released from jail through the efforts of the new minister to France, James Monroe. Broken in health, his hair white at fifty-seven, he wrote bitterly to Washington, "In the progress of events you beheld yourself a president in America and me a prisoner in France; you folded your arms, forgot your friend, and became silent." He openly branded Washington "a hypocrite in public life." His attacks on the patriot already being revered as "Father of his Country" only added to the horror with which most Americans held Tom Paine.

In 1802 "the Devil's disciple" returned to America at the courageous invitation of a man who remained his staunch friend and admirer. Thomas Jefferson was now President of the United States he and Paine had helped to create.

Ailing, tired, drinking too much, Paine visited the Executive Mansion as an honored guest. Jefferson offered him a government post. Paine refused because he didn't want Jefferson crucified any more on his account. The Federalist press was roaring angrily, "Let Jefferson and his blasphemous crony dangle from the same gallows!"

Denounced on all sides in press and pulpit, Paine fought back with a series of *Letters to the Citizens of the United States.* He reminded Americans of his role in the Revolution and that it was he who had first urged strong federal union. He repeated his bitter charges against Washington—"he accepted as a present a hundred thousand acres in America, and left me to occupy six foot of earth in France." And he stood firm in his criticism of organized Christianity as the enemy of free religious thought.

Urged by his few remaining friends to be silent before his reputation was utterly ruined, Paine wrote defiantly, "In taking up any public matter, I have never made it a consideration, and never will, whether it be popular or unpopular; but whether it be *right* or *wrong.*"

Americans cursed openly in the streets at the man who had named the United States of America. Mobs gathered to jeer at him; stagecoach owners refused to transport him; election supervisors challenged his right to vote. The embattled patriot sank into a slough of despair, justifying at last the calumnies of his enemies by falling into an alcoholism that left him often sodden and disheveled.

He died in New York City on June 8, 1809.

History textbooks are sometimes curiously brief about Tom Paine's great contributions to the American Revolution. Some authors are embarrassed by the legend of Paine as "atheistic drunkard and low fellow." Others cannot or dare not forgive his attacks on Washington and organized religion.

But time itself has vindicated Paine's fiery crusades against privilege, for the revolutionary overturn of tyranny, for democracy, against dishonesty by public officials, for the rights of man, for a strong federal union, for the appeal to reason over prejudice. Nor is it any longer considered shocking to suggest that Washington, or any other American President, had some human frailties.

And today it is no longer considered heretical to question rigid religious orthodoxy. Modern ministers, priests, and rabbis are now freely reexamining church doctrine, just as Paine dared to do. Much dogma is being discarded or revised, with a new emphasis upon the original spirit of Christianity and Judaism rather than upon forms of worship.

The Unitarian Church in America, founded in America a dozen years before his death, reflects many of Tom Paine's ideas about man's relationship to God.

4

The Common Scold

Anne Royall

Washington had never heard anything like it. Anne Royall would be the first American woman tried for the crime of being "a Common Scold." Prosecuted under an obsolete English law, she faced a unique punishment—being tied to a ducking stool and submerged under a pool of water. The case of the United States versus Anne Royall came to trial in Washington's Circuit Court in May 1829.

The prosecution presented a dozen witnesses to testify that the defendant had talked abusively in public to members of a Presbyterian congregation meeting in a firehouse near her home. One Captain John Coyle claimed she had called him "a damned old baldheaded——." Chief Librarian of Congress Henry Watterson testified that she had called all Presbyterians "cutthroats." A third witness charged that she had humiliated his sister by referring to her as an "old maid."

Anne Royall saw the trial as a plot to punish her for speaking and writing scornfully about the first religious revival crusade in America. Presbyterians were being sent into the Bible Belt as home missionaries to convert Indians, infidels, and members of other sects. Anne Royall, a hot-tempered, outspoken woman who traveled widely and wrote books about what she saw, had been a thorn in their side.

Mocking them as "Holy Willies" and their women as "Miss Dismals," she charged them with "contaminating" the Indians, lobbying for federal funds to support church schools, and attempting to win a privileged government position for Presbyterianism.

The courtroom was jammed as Anne Royall gave her version of the events that had led to her indictment as a "Common Scold." She testified that she had complained to the congregation about their constant, loud hymn singing next door, branding it a public nuisance. In reprisal, she said, children had been encouraged to throw rocks at her home.

Then Captain Coyle, a congregation leader, had stood under her window, praying loudly for the salvation of her soul. His hypocrisy infuriated her, she testified, because she knew him to be the secret father of her maid's child. That was when she had broadcast her opinion of the Evangelicals.

Senator John Eaton of Tennessee, later Secretary of War, took the stand to testify to Anne Royall's good character.

But the jury brought in a verdict of guilty.

When the moment came for her punishment, a ducking stool specially constructed by carpenters in the Alexandria Navy Yard was brought into the courthouse square. The three Circuit Court judges, staring at the monstrosity, found themselves unable to order a woman strapped into it and publicly plunged into a bath of cold water. Instead, they summoned Anne Royall to the bench and substituted a ten-dollar fine. She also had to post a fifty-dollar bond as a pledge to keep the peace.

Although she had escaped the ducking stool, Anne Royall knew that her enemies had won their objective. They had hurt her reputation, branded her a character assassin, and crippled the sale of her books, on which she depended for a modest living. Exhausted and made ill by the strain of the trial, she gave up her travels and sought a new livelihood.

Traveling through the nation as America's first woman journalist, Anne Royall reported candidly on the flaws and blemishes of her countrymen as she saw them. Even after the ducking stool trial had brought her low, she rose again to a prominence that won her interviews with seven presidents, from Martin Van Buren to Franklin Pierce.

She was born Anne Newport in Maryland on June 11, 1769. After the Revolution her father, a Tory sympathizer, was forced to move to the Pennsylvania frontier, where Anne lived a rugged pioneer life until she was thirteen. When Indian raids killed both her father and a stepfather, she and her mother wandered south to Staunton, Virginia.

They were rescued from dire poverty by the generosity of Captain William Royall, a former officer in the Revolutionary Army. He gave them jobs on the Sweet Springs plantation he owned—Anne worked as a servant, her mother as laundress. A charitable Freemason, William Royall gave Anne advice she never forgot: "If ever you find yourself in trouble, appeal to a Mason."

Undertaking her education himself, he taught her to read and write. Then he turned her loose in his large personal library to study thinkers like Voltaire, Paine, and Jefferson. Finally, when Anne was twenty-eight, he proposed to her. They were married that same afternoon, November 18, 1797.

Their marriage was a happy one. When Royall died in 1813, his will left everything to Anne. Angry relatives contested it, and litigation over the estate dragged out for ten dreary years. Meanwhile, Anne decided to broaden herself by travel.

"Hitherto, I have only learned mankind in theory—but now I am studying him in practise," she wrote in her travel journal. "One learns more in a day by mixing with mankind than he can in an age shut up in a closet." For five years, traveling in a carriage with a driver, two men slaves, and a maid, she explored, with an insatiable curiosity, newly settled states and territories of the South.

In 1823 word reached her that the courts had decided her husband's will in favor of the other relatives. Overnight, from thinking herself a rich widow, she found herself suddenly as threadbare poor as when she had first arrived at Sweet Springs as a servant girl. She was now fifty-four and in ill health.

Anne decided to go to Washington and apply for a pension as the widow of an officer of the American Revolution. To divert herself from brooding over her misfortunes, she jotted down observations on her journey.

Traveling without money, she was indebted to strangers for her stage fare. She slept where she could, eating scraps thrown out from tavern kitchens. She also did not hesitate to approach Masons, who never failed to offer her food, quarters, and clothes. One Mason, a hotel proprietor in Alexandria, provided her with a room and servant for the winter.

Reaching Richmond to search war records for proof of her husband's military career, she found they had been lost in a city fire. Still destitute, she begged money from passersby, quoting passages from the Bible to inspire Christian charity. They ignored her. Finally she met a Mason who gave her the money she needed to continue on to Washington.

Here, a random knock on a house door won her the hospitality of a family named Dorret, who gave her board and lodging for six months "without fee or reward," and supplied new clothes to replace her threadbare garments. Here, while trying to win a war widow's pension, she began making her travel notes into a book, *Sketches of History, Life and Manners in the United States.*

She managed to see John Quincy Adams, then Secretary of State under President Monroe, and persuade him to present her pension petition himself. He also paid five dollars in advance for a copy of *Sketches.* To collect other orders and more material to finish the book, Anne set off on new travels through Pennsylvania, New York, and New England.

She traveled any way she could—jolting on abominable roads in springless, iron-tired stagecoaches; posting on horseback; freezing on riverboats; trudging on foot along dusty back roads; rowing herself along winding streams. She probably saw more of both rustic and urban America and its citizens than any woman of her time. Her sharp observations held a mirror up to the nation that outraged many Americans but provoked others to thoughtful discussion.

"Sometimes she lets fall more truths than the interested reader would wish to hear," commented the *Boston Commercial.* She accused Philadelphia, even then priding itself as the City of Brotherly Love, of being "unfeeling, inhospitable and uncharitable toward strangers." She saw the city, whose Quakers had refused to take up arms in the Revolution, as "a den of British tories, domestic traitors, missionaries and Sunday schoolism." Philadelphia ladies repelled Anne by their "eclat, hauteur or repelling stiffness"—except for one who was, instead, "a savage in petticoats."

New Yorkers, she found, "lay no claim to taste or refinement; their attention to business . . . leaves them no time to cultivate the graces." The women were stylish with vacant stares, unread because of a choice of too many amusements, devoting far more thought to dress than to books. Anne ironically credited them with one special talent—an elegant, graceful walk. "This excellence is attributed to their smooth paved Broadway, upon which they practise walking to a degree . . . crowned with success."

She praised Bostonians as literate, patriotic, nourished in "the soil of human excellence." Boston ladies, she declared, improved their minds, thus giving "ease to their manners, and an intelligence of countenance." A Boston chambermaid "will read as correct as the most finished scholar."

Visiting Hartford, Anne found its "crowning glory" to be the American Asylum for the Deaf and Dumb. "I would advise all gentlemen who wish to avoid a scolding wife, to go to the American Asylum where, I can assure them, they will find a good deal of good sense as well as beauty."

In Providence, while approving of the ideals of founder Roger Williams, she felt compelled to point out, "The churches are very splendid; the jail is tolerable; but the poorhouse does not deserve the name, and the hospital is a wretched abode, disgraceful to the town."

Her opinion of Southern cities and people was even less flattering. Charleston, South Carolina, was "the receptacle for the refuse of all nations on earth—the only reputable people there are the Jews." North Carolina ladies took snuff. Women in Washington and Baltimore were the worst dressed in America, and Baltimore's ladies were "illiterate, proud and ignorant," unable to read anything more than dream books.

Her travels during John Quincy Adams's administration (1825–29) reflected his frustration at being unable to get Congress to pass a bill authorizing federal aid for building local roads and schools. In Virginia, Anne reported, "the roads were as bad as the schools."

Her major complaint in most American communities she visited was the ignorance of even the most well-to-do women and the excessive drinking of even the most well-to-do men.

"There is too much whiskey everywhere," she wrote.

Her books offered candid appraisals of prominent Americans she met. She wrote of Congressman John Randolph of Virginia, "His voice is loud and shrill. . . . He is said to be immensely rich but not charitable." One apoplectic Brigadier General tried to buy up and destroy the books in which she described encountering a five-foot baboon she thought belonged to the General, only to find that it *was* the General.

Anne Royall trudged persistently around all the important villages, towns, and cities of that early United States, in all kinds of weather, taking notes, interviewing, soliciting orders for her books and delivering them. Once her feet began to bleed after walking around Philadelphia's cobbled streets from dawn to dusk. "I may as well walk to death," she shrugged, "as starve to death if I don't."

Often without enough clothes to keep her warm, she would write her books shivering in the dingy bedrooms of second-class taverns, her candle burning long after midnight.

In 1827, the Masonic Order sought out Anne Royall to ask her help. Masons were in deep trouble as the result of the murder the year before of an ex-Mason who had threatened to write an expose of the Masonic secret ritual. The affair had caused a national uproar. Despite Masonic protests of innocence, demagogic politicians had denounced Freemasonry as a bloodthirsty conspiracy like today's Mafia. An anti-Mason political party had formed, with its own Presidential candidate. Masonic lodges had been forced to shut down in many states.

The Masons knew Anne Royall as a staunch admirer of Masonry, the widow of a Mason, and a woman of influence through her books. They offered to finance her travels if she would also incorporate Masonic propaganda in her books. She agreed promptly. Their grant took her through almost every section of the United States for the next three years and subsidized four of the nine books that she wrote.

Critics charged that she had "sold herself to the Masons." She had—but only because she sincerely believed in Masonry. Years later in Washington, offered a two-thousand-dollar bribe by President Jackson's political enemies to suppress a news story exposing them, she refused even though the little paper she was publishing then kept her poor to the point of hunger. "Some people think we write for pay, and so we do," she declared proudly, "but we are not an hireling writer."

She did much to quiet anti-Masonic hysteria. Washington, Franklin, and New York's Governor De Witt Clinton were Masons, she pointed out. Would such great Americans have joined an ugly, terroristic, anti-church conspiracy? She related how often so-called Christians had turned their backs on her when she was hungry, but never the Masons.

"If it were not for Masonry," she wrote in a burst of grateful fervor, "the world would become a herd of savages!"

Two days after Christmas 1827, she called on a Burlington, Vermont, storekeeper to sell her books. "Get to the workhouse where you belong, you Masons!" he swore.

As she related it, "He took hold of me with a hand on each shoulder and pushed me with such force that he sent me to the foot of the steps into the street. My ankle was dislocated, one of the bones of the same leg broken, and the whole limb bruised and mangled in the most shocking manner."

It took three years before she could walk again without limping. Her challenge to anti-Masons grew more defiant.

"If Morgan was murdered, what of it?" she demanded. "How many men are murdered daily without ascertaining by whom? . . . If they cannot find the murderer, with all the police force of the country to ferret out the crime, they are not very smart. This Morgan story is precisely like the witches of Salem . . . a Missionary scheme to raise money."

A Masonic procession in 1793, with George Washington standing under the crossed spears.

This was a period of fanatical Calvinism or Evangelicalism, when the American Home Missionary Society began spreading a fire-and-brimstone Puritanism that had driven Roger Williams out of the Massachusetts colony two hundred years earlier.

"Alas!" Anne Royall wrote, "when will the long catalogue be filled of the unfortunate victims of the impious and cruel dogmas of AN IMPLACABLE GOD, AN OMNIPOTENT DEVIL, AND AN ENDLESS HELL? Never, until these horrid dogmas are banished from the earth!"

She fought the Evangelical lobby's attempt to win free mail franking for their tracts, and attacked missionary attempts to convert Indians as hypocritical. "There was not a more upright, noble or virtuous people on the globe, or one possessed of a higher sense of honor than the aborigines of America until they were contaminated by the missionaries!"

She was highly unpopular with the Evangelicals for revealing that missionaries were allowed to keep 10 percent of donations they collected. They fumed when she taunted: "I am one of those heathen you are so anxious to convert . . . the Bible was put into my hands. But I watched the conduct of those who read it, and I found they committed murder, they robbed, they got drunk, they betrayed their friends and were guilty of all kinds of abominations, and I was afraid to read the Bible lest I might do so too."

The Montgomery, Alabama, *Journal* acknowledged, "She is doing much good in opposition to fanaticism." But Anne Royall's enemies finally won their revenge by forcing her trial and conviction as a "Common Scold," even though they failed in their effort to humiliate her on a ducking stool.

Now sixty-three, she decided to stay in Washington and put out her own four-page weekly. It appeared first as *Paul Pry* on December 3, 1831; she changed its name five years later to *The Huntress.* Her paper was promptly attacked by the *New England Religious Weekly* for containing "all the scum, billingsgate and filth extant" that might be expected from "a convicted Common Scold." Anne Royall asked dryly, "Wonder in what part of the Bible they found that?"

Few women of her time were as deeply engrossed in major political issues of the day. Like Jackson, she firmly opposed the Bank of the United States as a monopoly designed to benefit the rich at the expense of the poor. She predicted he would veto Congress's renewal of its charter. Jackson did. An infuriated Bank stockholder assaulted her with a thick walking stick. "Only the fact that I had on a heavily wadded bonnet . . . saved my life," she reported.

When John Quincy Adams became President, she learned that he took dawn swims in the Potomac. Turning up one dawn on the riverbank, she sat on his clothes until he agreed to give her a statement of his views on the Bank. "She is a virago errant in enchanted armor," Adams grinned later.

Her little paper crusaded for new causes along with the old—against flogging in the Navy, fraud in the Post Office, land company swindles of the Indians; for better labor conditions, free speech, separation of church and state, territorial expansion, and unrestricted immigration.

When Catholic immigration grew heavy in 1837, she fought a rising tide of anti-Catholic sentiment by reminding her fellow Americans, "A Catholic foreigner discovered America. Catholic foreigners first settled it. . . . At present, we verily believe that the liberty of this country is in more danger from natives than from foreigners!"

An enthusiastic supporter of new inventions, she chastised Congress for not rewarding Morse for inventing the telegraph; and urged women to submit to the new daguerreotype machine that would take their pictures: "It requires but a few minutes to take a likeness. You have nothing to do but sit still upon your chair and look through a tube. . . . No lady need apprehend the least thing unpleasant. . . . To us it appears superhuman, and among our greatest discoveries."

When she was seventy-nine, Congress finally granted her a war widow's pension in the lump sum of twelve hundred dollars, which dwindled to three dollars when she paid off all her debts. She lived another six years on the edge of starvation, surviving largely through the generosity of admiring Masons, Unitarians, Catholics, and Jews.

At eighty-five she was invited to the White House to interview her seventh President, Franklin Pierce. On July 2, 1854, she wrote her last editorial, declaring her trust in Heaven for three things—that, with only thirty-one cents on hand, subscribers would pay what they owed so that she could pay the printer and her rent; that Washington would escape the rampant cholera epidemic; and that, despite the growing rift between North and South, "the UNION OF THESE STATES MAY BE ETERNAL."

Dying three months later, she was buried in an unmarked grave in the Congressional Cemetery because there was no money for a tombstone. "To the hour of her death," observed the *Washington Star*, "she preserved all the peculiarities of thought, temper and manners, which at one time rendered her so famous throughout the land."

In an era when ladies were supposed to behave with strict propriety, leaving the heavy thinking to men while they devoted themselves to piety, clothes, and "an elegant, graceful walk," Anne Royall showed that women could be intellectual, independent, and as bold as men in the pursuit of principles. In her inimitable fashion, she paved the way for suffragettes, women newspaper correspondents, lady doctors, women in politics, and other female emancipationists.

Her books remain valuable contributions to the social history of the United States. For her courage in telling Americans the truth about themselves as she saw it, she was denounced as a crank and sentenced to a ducking stool as a Common Scold. Outraged males assaulted her twice.

But she persevered and established a literary tradition of candid, American self-criticism, later followed by such giants of American letters as Horace Greeley, Henry David Thoreau, Lincoln Steffens, Upton Sinclair, Theodore Dreiser, Sinclair Lewis, and H. L. Mencken—all "Common Scolds."

5

The Beatnik of 1830

Joseph Palmer

People on the streets of Fitchburg, Massachusetts, gaped at him in astonishment. Clustering irresistibly in his wake, they exchanged eager guesses about his identity.

One citizen was sure he was one of the new German refugees who had fled to America from an abortive uprising.

"No, he's one of them Latter-day Saints from them disgraceful hay-reems over in Fayette, New York." A Fitchburg housewife threw a baleful glance after the stranger. "Mormon! Hairy goats prancing after concubines!"

A schoolmaster guessed him to be a Grahamite, one of the "Nature people" who ate only whole wheat and vegetables.

"Don't you know what it is?" scoffed a gangling adolescent. "It's a Jew! They're the ones what wears whiskers!"

Beards had not been seen on men's faces in the United States for almost a hundred years. America's heroes—Washington, Jefferson, Franklin, Ethan Allen, Hamilton, John Adams, all the signers of the Declaration of Independence—had all been gentlemen with smooth faces.

But that example apparently was not good enough for the stranger who had suddenly appeared on the streets of Fitchburg wearing an enormous, flowing beard. The likes of such majestic whiskers had never been seen outside Old Testament illustrations. Joseph Palmer was a forty-two-year-old farmer who had

moved with his wife and son from a nearby hamlet to the growing village of Fitchburg. Far from being a newcomer to America, he was a descendant of original New England settlers. His
father had fought in the Revolutionary Army, and he himself
had fought for America in the War of 1812.

Why, then, had he chosen to be different from everyone else in
America and wear a huge beard? One of the first people in Fitchburg to ask that question bluntly was the local pastor, Reverend
George Trask. He was surprised to find that Palmer was no uncouth
fool but an extremely well-read, thoughtful, deeply religious man.

"Reverend," Palmer replied gently, "have you forgotten that
the bearded Nazarite was the holiest of men, set aside to serve
God and set an example? We are told in the Book of Numbers,
Chapter 6, Verse 5, 'All the days of the vow of his separation
there shall no razor come upon his head . . . and shall let the
locks of the hair of his head grow.'"

Palmer also cited Leviticus, Chapter 21, Verse 5, where God
instructed the holy, "They shall not make baldness upon their
head, neither shall they shave off the corner of their beard." And
Proverbs, Chapter 16, Verse 31: "The hoary head is a crown of
glory, if it be found in the way of righteousness."

He smiled wanly. "So you see, Reverend, it would be more
appropriate for me to ask why *you,* as a holier man than I, do *not*
obey Scriptures and wear a beard."

Mouth open, the Reverend Trask blinked. "But those are the
ways of olden times, friend," he stammered.

"God's word is never out of fashion with me, Reverend.
Would the Lord have given men whiskers if he did not mean
us to wear them? It was not God who created razors, but men."

Joseph Palmer preferred to live as he believed God intended
him to, even though he was the only man in the United States
to do so. But he soon began to pay heavily for his refusal to
conform. Stones crashing through the windows of his modest
farmhouse expressed the indignation of townspeople over his

uncouth appearance. Small boys hooted and flung mud after "old Jew Palmer" and tormented his son at school. Villagers mocked him to his face. When his wife appeared in town, other women turned their backs on her.

"You should be prosecuted for wearing such a monstrosity!" old Doctor Williams snapped at Palmer one day. A group of men around him chorused angry agreement.

Palmer faced them calmly. "This is a free country. I am a law-abiding citizen and I have done no harm to anyone. If I wish to wear a beard, that is entirely my right."

"Don't be too sure!" one of the men snarled.

In church, members of the congregation pointedly sat as far away from the Palmer family as possible. But he refused to miss a Sunday's worship. On a communion Sunday in 1830, an incident occurred that plunged the town into an uproar.

As the officiating clergyman approached with the communion bread and wine, Palmer and his family kneeled with other worshipers bowing their heads. But to Palmer's amazement, the prelate deliberately passed them by, moving on to the next parishioner. Palmer's self-restraint tore loose, less at the insult to himself than to his wife and son.

Rising from his knees, he strode to the communion table and emptied the cup at one giant swig. Voice trembling with fury, he thundered at the congregation, "I love my Jesus as well—and better—than any of you!" Then he swept up his family and stormed out of the church.

The next few days were marked by a great deal of cabalistic whispering in Fitchburg. There was unanimous agreement about what had to be done. One afternoon as Palmer emerged from Fitchburg House in the center of town, he became aware of four men lounging furtively at the street corner.

As he sought to pass by, two men suddenly flung themselves on him, pinning his hands behind his back. One man produced a box with scissors, soap, brush, and razor.

"Palmer," he said grimly, "it is the solid opinion of the citizens of Fitchburg that your whiskers are an insult to the eye. Since you don't have the common decency to shave them off, we have been selected to do it for you!"

Palmer's eyes became black flames.

"You'll have to kill me first," he vowed.

The man with the scissors grabbed his beard. Palmer struggled with a wild fury that flung off his assailants. All four men then attacked him and threw him violently to the ground, injuring his back. They held him down, but he still refused to be subdued. As the man with the scissors tried to slash his beard, Palmer tore one arm free. Getting a knife out of his pocket, he whipped it around him.

Two assailants sprang back howling with dismay and anguish at painful, but not serious, slashes in their legs.

Palmer leaped to his feet, back hurt, cheeks bleeding, clothes torn—but beard untouched. He held the knife up grimly in a defensive position. But the four would-be barbers had had enough of trying to beard a lion, and fled.

The village was far from through with him, however. His four assailants promptly filed a complaint against him for "unprovoked assault." The Sheriff of Worcester arrested Palmer and led him off to the county seat for trial. In court he admitted having defended himself with a knife, pointing out that the unprovoked assault had come from the four plaintiffs, not from him. But Justice Brigham, glaring distastefully at the defendant's beard, found him guilty and fined him.

Palmer refused to pay the fine.

"You'll pay it," the judge snapped, "or go to jail!"

"Put me in jail, then. It's a matter of principle."

Justice Brigham almost choked in his fury. "We'll see! Sheriff, lock this man in jail—and *keep* him there until his fine is paid to this Court!"

For over a year Joseph Palmer was kept in the county jail at Worcester for the crime of having resisted a forcible attempt to shave off his beard. Nor was he safe even in jail. His jailer, a sadistic brute named Bellows, enlisted two cronies in another attempt to separate Palmer from his beard. He fought them off so savagely that they were forced to retreat, and he was punished by being put into solitary confinement.

His beard then became a tempting trophy to other prisoners, who made two attempts to strip him of it. Each time he beat them off, Bellows flung him into solitary again.

Palmer protested the miserable food, the rat-ridden cells, the refusal to let his wife and son visit him, the lack of a visiting minister or a prison chapel. Bellows and the Sheriff laughed at eccentric "Old Whiskers," who apparently thought that jail was "some manner of luxurious inn."

Palmer's son, Thomas, smuggled paper and pencil to him through the window of his cell. The prisoner wrote a series of moving letters describing his plight, dropping them over the walls to his son. Thomas took them to the editor of the Worcester *Spy*, who was impressed enough to publish them. They quickly attracted the attention of other editors, and were widely reprinted throughout Massachusetts.

In the letters Palmer protested that he had been imprisoned unjustly, not for "unprovoked assault," but for insisting upon his right to wear a beard. He complained of conditions in the Worcester jail, and deplored above all the starvation of his soul for lack of a religious life.

His letters lit a bonfire of indignation. Could it really be true that such persecution of a God-fearing Christian could be going on, in the year of our Lord 1831, in the state founded by victims of religious persecution? What state or town law against wearing beards had the prisoner violated? Did not the people of Fitchburg, and the judge, Sheriff, and jailer of Worcester, know that it was a man's Constitutional right to groom himself any way he liked?

A storm of protest swept down on the alarmed legal authorities of Worcester. Joseph Palmer could no longer be pushed around contemptuously as a comic figure, religious fanatic, or eccentric crank. Editorials hailed "the Bearded Prisoner of Worcester" as a courageous martyr, a majestic one-man symbol of the Bill of Rights embattled.

The nervous Sheriff consulted Justice Brigham, who hastily agreed to free Palmer before the indignation of an aroused citizenry swept them both out of public office. Then the Sheriff hurried to the jail and entered Palmer's cell.

"I bring you good news," he told the prisoner cheerfully, clapping a hand on his shoulder. "I have finally persuaded Justice Brigham to pardon you. You have certainly been here long enough. You are free to go home now and forget the whole thing. The fine and everything!"

The bearded man folded his arms. "I reject your pardon. I have done nothing to be pardoned for. I did not ask to be brought here. I will not cooperate in any way with your act of injustice." He refused to walk out of the cell.

The Sheriff's jaw dropped in chagrin. The sadistic jailer Bellows snarled at Palmer not to be a fool. He'd been yelling about being kept from his wife, son, and church, hadn't he? Well, he was free to go to them now, wasn't he?

Palmer ignored him. "If my remaining true to principle results in a state investigation," he told the Sheriff, "that is your problem, sir, not mine."

The Sheriff turned pale. "We'll see about that!"

Palmer's aged mother was induced to write a pitiful letter urging her son to leave jail and come home to see her. The bearded prisoner choked with emotion but refused to budge. Justice Brigham himself came to prison to plead with him.

"I won't walk a single step toward the freedom I was deprived of unjustly," Palmer replied. "I can preach the gospel of freedom to more Americans by staying where you put me than I can anywhere else."

Jailer Bellows hissed that if he insisted on staying locked up, they might put him back in solitary confinement.

"It was never solitary confinement," Palmer said calmly. "God was always present in the cell with me."

In despair Justice Brigham gave the Sheriff an ultimatum— either Palmer was to be turned out or the Sheriff's badge was to be turned in. So the Sheriff, some deputies, and jailer Bellows entered the bearded man's cell with a chair. He offered no resistance as they forced him to sit down in it. Folding his arms across his chest, he went limp in passive non-resistance, just as civil rights and peace demonstrators were to do over a century later when police laid hands upon them for refusing to disperse.

"Since you won't leave jail voluntarily," the Sheriff blustered, "we'll *carry* you out!" Smiling quietly in triumph, Joseph Palmer was picked up in the chair and carried out of the Worcester jail. They dumped him in the street outside and left him. Rising with the dignity of a Christian martyr freed from the dungeons of the Coliseum, he calmly made his way home—the only man in American history who had had to be thrown *out* of prison as well as in.

No one ever again dared torment, mock, or lay hands upon the thorny Joseph Palmer, whose championship of beards had become famous throughout the Eastern seaboard. Due partly to his influence and new prestige, beards slowly began to come back in style in American life. Traveling medicine men began peddling beard-growers guaranteed to stimulate magnificent whiskers as symbols of manliness. By the 1860s prominent Americans were almost all bearded—Abraham Lincoln, Stonewall Jackson, Jefferson Davis, Ulysses S. Grant, Robert E. Lee, Horace Greeley, Walt Whitman.

After being freed in 1831, Palmer joined the abolitionists in fighting slavery. He became a friend of other highly individualistic idealists like Thoreau, Emerson, and Alcott. When intellectuals set up co-operative colonies as Utopian experiments, he helped plow their fields. He also supported temperance societies, convinced that intoxication was not only ungodly, but led Americans to the kind of senseless excesses that had resulted in his own persecution.

On his deathbed in 1875, he had only to look about him to see a whole nation transformed into men with beards, in large part due to his own stubborn courage. He was buried in North Leominster, Massachusetts, not far from the infamous Worcester county jail. His tombstone proclaimed: Joseph Palmer, persecuted for wearing the beard. Above it rose a carving of his majestic head with flowing beard, beautifully and reverently executed in white marble.

Like Joseph Palmer in 1830, thousands of Americans today—particularly young men known as beatniks and hippies—have been subjected to pressure and harassment because of their non-conformist appearance, especially the wearing of beards in an America once more largely clean-shaven.

Their reasons are seldom scriptural, like Palmer's, but they do find a sense of spiritual exaltation in wearing beards as an expression of individuality in a society that they criticize as too conformist and regimented.

One bearded employee of the Atlanta Construction Department was fired in 1967 by the same department head who had recommended him for permanent civil service status, because he had grown the beard after being rated "entirely satisfactory." The American Civil Liberties Union forced Atlanta to rehire him by proving he had been discriminated against.

A Pasadena high school teacher who refused to shave off his beard that same year was stripped of his right to teach classes. When the ACLU fought his case in court, his right to wear a beard, under the First and Fourteenth Amendments, was upheld unanimously by the California State Court of Appeals.

"It seems to us," the Court stated, "that the wearing of a beard is a form of expression of an individual's personality, and that such a right of expression, although probably not within the literal scope of the First Amendment, is . . . entitled to its peripheral protection."

In 1967, too, some two hundred hippies were ordered to leave New York's Tompkins Square Park because they refused to obey a police sergeant's order to stop their music and noisemaking. They stood their ground, showing a New York City Parks Department permit allowing them to hold a meeting there. Forty hippies were arrested. In court one officer testified that the police sergeant had instructed him to arrest five people.

"Any five?" asked the judge incredulously.

"Yes," admitted the officer sheepishly. "Any five."

The indignant judge dismissed the charges, declaring firmly, "This Court will not deny the equal protection of the law to the unwashed, unshod, unkempt, and uninhibited."

Joseph Palmer is dead, but his soul goes marching on.

6

"Burn the Tribune! Hang Old Greeley!"

Horace Greeley

Horace Greeley looked up as a large brick suddenly crashed through the window next to his desk. His managing editor, Sidney Gay, came bursting into his office. "For God's sake, sir, you must leave the city at once! Use the back door. They mean to kill you. It's no riot—it's a revolution!"

Over drooping spectacles, Greeley stared out at the shouting mobs below. He was a dumpy, owl-faced man with a fringe of wild white hair, his clothes always rumpled and disarrayed. He had known there would be riots after the huge peace party mass meeting in June. Mayor Fernando Wood had inflamed New York City's poor workers against a new federal draft law that allowed rich men to buy substitutes to serve for them in the Army. And Irish-American laborers were furious at the *Tribune* for crusading for emancipation, blaming Greeley for the freed slaves who were brought to New York and used as strikebreakers.

The last straw was the bloody Battle of Gettysburg with over 23,000 Union casualties—23,000 spaces in the ranks that a new draft call had to fill. Anti-draft riots broke out on July 11, 1863. Crowds poured through the streets, burning buildings, hanging Negroes from lamp posts, tearing up tracks, overturning horsecars. The *Tribune,* a national symbol of the fight against slavery, became a prime target of mob fury. Thousands stormed into Printing House Square, advancing on the five-story *Tribune* building across from City Hall.

"Burn the *Tribune!*" they roared. "Hang old Greeley!"

The fifty-two-year-old editor said calmly, "I have no doubt they do indeed mean to hang me. Well, it doesn't make much difference. I've done my work. I may as well be killed by this mob as die in my bed. Between now and the next time is only a little while." He looked at his watch. "Hm, worked past my dinner time. I'm going out to eat."

"My God, Mr. Greeley, they'll tear you to pieces!"

"If I can't eat my dinner when I'm hungry, what use is life to me anyhow?" He slapped on the disreputable old white hat and duster that would make him a marked man to the frenzied rioters now surging against police lines. Then he ambled out the front door and straight into the astonished mob.

There was a sudden, dazed silence. The awed rioters closest to him fell back, opening a path for the legendary crusader. Untouched, he made his way to a nearby restaurant. Then the mob smashed into the ground floor of the *Tribune* and had to be dispersed by Army troops. In three days of rioting, a thousand New Yorkers were killed or wounded.

The nation read about it in Horace Greeley's paper.

Born to a poverty-stricken farm couple of Amherst, New Hampshire, on February 3, 1811, he saw the family farm foreclosed and his father forced to flee debtors' prison. Probably because of these events he became a champion of the poor and oppressed, and a fearless opponent of the powerful and respectable.

A child prodigy who had read through the Bible at five, he began his career as a printer's apprentice. By twenty-three he was in New York City publishing a weekly for intelligent readers, *The New Yorker.* Refusing to print claptrap to increase his circulation, he was constantly on the edge of bankruptcy. When

Thousands of rioters stormed the Tribune building.

a seven-year depression began in 1834, he outraged business-men and church leaders by accusing them of indifference to the sufferings of the poor, who were dying in the slums that winter of hunger and pneumonia, and by suggesting that they see to it that every man who needed a job was given one.

"Morality and religion are but words," he wrote bitterly, "to him who fishes in gutters for the means of sustaining life, and crouches behind barrels in the street for shelter from the cutting blasts of a winter night."

He warned the unemployed to abandon the cities: "Fly—scatter through the land—go to the Great West!" It was the first of many exhortations later to become famous as the Greeley credo: "Go West, young man, go West!"

His brilliance as an editorialist brought New York State Whig leader, Thurlow Weed, to him for help in electing William

Seward as Governor in 1838. A Whig follower of Henry Clay, Greeley agreed to divide his time between *The New Yorker* and a new, temporary political paper, the *Jeffersonian.*

"You are now a member of the 'firm' of Seward, Weed and Greeley," Weed assured him. The *Jeffersonian* proved highly persuasive. Seward became Governor, and Weed boss of New York State politics. Too proud to ask for a reward, Greeley hoped for a political appointment that would help him get out of debt. But Seward and Weed simply forgot about him.

He turned his attention back to his personal crusades.

The sixty-day jail term for blasphemy of an ex-clergyman turned atheist provoked a blast at the Boston magistrate who inflicted it. When troops were rushed to Georgia to punish a Cherokee tribe for executing two government agents who had defrauded them, Greeley accused the United States Indian Bureau as "the real murderers." Upon an attack by state troops on Mormons settling in Missouri, he labeled Missouri "a disgrace to the Union." High-handed public officials hated the outspoken crusader and dreaded the whiplash of his scorn.

Despite Whig Boss Weed's failure to show appreciation for his help in electing Seward governor, Greeley agreed to mastermind Weed's campaign to elect William Henry Harrison as the first Whig President in 1840. His hoopla with the slogan "Tippecanoe and Tyler, Too," selling Harrison as a log cabin pioneer who became the Indian-fighting hero of the Battle of Tippecanoe, won the White House for the Whigs.

Only twenty-nine, Greeley found himself exhilarated by the immense power he had wielded. But despite the fact that no man in the nation had contributed more to the Whigs' victory, Boss Weed and Governor Seward both again turned deaf ears to any suggestions that Greeley be given a political appointment. The firm of "Seward, Weed and Greeley," the editor reflected wryly, operated only when they needed him.

In 1841 Greeley met reformer Arthur Brisbane, who interested him in Fourierism—a Utopian movement that urged collective, self-sustaining colonies of four or five hundred families each as an answer to unemployment and poverty. Seeing Fourierism as a plan for reorganizing American society, Greeley advocated it enthusiastically in *The New Yorker* and the *Tribune,* which he started on April 10, 1841, as a four-page penny daily. He was widely denounced for fostering Socialism.

"When I took up this cause," he told the first Fourierist Convention a few years later, "I knew that I went in the teeth of many of my patrons, in the teeth of the prejudices of the great mass, in the teeth of religious prejudices. I confess I had a great many more clergymen on my subscription list before than I have now."

Helping to found the Sylvania Phalanx in Pennsylvania, he was rueful when it went bankrupt like most of the other Fourierist experiments. They had, he sighed, "that communistic basis which seems calculated to prove fatal." He told Brisbane he had become convinced Fourierism could only work when it had a religious basis, like the Shaker colony.

Brisbane expressed surprise that Greeley, so often denounced as an atheist, considered himself religious.

"Indeed I am, Brisbane," Greeley nodded. "I'm a Universalist. We believe that God is too good to damn us—unlike Unitarians, who think they're too good to be damned!"

His new penny daily, the *Tribune,* proved an immediate success. Greeley began to feud with other editors in circulation duels. When the *Sun's* publisher ordered its newsboys to beat up the *Tribune's* hawkers, he promptly hired huskier boys to drive them off. He showed great ingenuity in scooping rivals on newsbeats. But he delighted readers most, as one of them put it, "because he makes you think—even when he gets you hopping mad!" People bought the *Tribune* to see what new outrageous idea "Uncle Horace" would propose next.

He advocated the right of women to vote, the abolition of capital punishment, prohibition, the right of men to jobs, the puddings of "health" flour developed by Dr. Sylvester Graham, free homesteads for the poor, legal limits to the amount of land any one man could own, an end to the smoking habit, and railroads to open up the West.

A generous man who could never refuse any appeal for money by those in need, he liked to pose as too cagey to have his heartstrings plucked, growling in print, "Two-thirds of those who beg from door to door, or who write begging letters, are the very last persons who ought to be given a shinplaster dime!" But he turned down only those he considered hypocrites, like the shocked cultist soliciting funds to publish pious tracts who protested, "But, Mr. Greeley, don't you want to save sinners from going to Hell?"

"No!" he snarled. "It isn't half full enough of them!"

He enjoyed dramatizing himself as a super eccentric, shrewdly believing that the more he shocked people as a "character," the more readers he would win for the *Tribune*. He even described himself as "tow-headed, and half-bald at that . . . slouching dress; goes bent like a hoop, and so rocking in his gait that he walks down both sides of the street at once." He was delighted when an admirer described him as "a man who could save a Nation, but never learn to tie a cravat."

Despite a squeaky, screechy, singsong, and shrill voice, he was in great demand as a lecturer. Henry Ward Beecher once asked him how he could tell when any lecture he gave was a success. "Well, Henry," Greeley said thoughtfully, "I guess it's when more folks stay in than go out."

When the Mexican War broke out, Greeley joined Abraham Lincoln, a new Whig Congressman from Illinois, in branding it as "unnecessarily and unconstitutionally begun by the President." Lincoln challenged Democratic President Polk to name the spot on American soil where blood was shed by any Mexican.

Polk irately condemned those who opposed the Mexican War as "unpatriotic."

In an angry editorial called *What Means This War?*, Greeley declared, "It means that the Commandments are to be read and obeyed by our People thus: Thou *shalt* kill Mexicans. Thou *shalt* steal from them, hate them, burn their houses, ravage their fields, and fire red-hot cannon balls into towns swarming with their wives and children." Greeley's indignation had future echoes in the Vietnam War protests of the 1960s.

He broke with the Whigs over Boss Weed's insistence on nominating General Zachary Taylor, slaveholder and Mexican War hero, as the party's Presidential candidate in 1848. To lure back his support, Weed let him finish the unexpired term— three months—of a Whig Congressman who had died.

Horace Greeley went to Washington, granted ninety precious days in which to turn America upside down. On his first day, he introduced a bill to stop land speculation and offer free homesteads to settlers. He exposed a bill as an attempt at Whig graft, and defeated it. He opposed slave trade, and then created an uproar by taking on the armed services.

He insisted that the Navy reduce its staff of officers, cut down on promotions, stop issuing liquor rations, and prohibit flogging as punishment. He tried to cut $38,000 out of an Army appropriations bill, accusing the Army of paying recruiters to get men drunk and enlist them in a stupor.

But the issue that really stirred up a hornet's nest was Greeley's accusation that Congressmen were cheating the American taxpayers by padding their expense accounts for travel. "Some Congressmen," he thundered, "are charging enough to travel from California to Washington by way of Siberia!" The House roared back, "Shame! Shame!" Greeley was denounced for including Congressman Abe Lincoln in his charges.

"Calling me a hypocrite or demagogue," he snapped back, "cannot make a charge of $1664 for coming to Congress from

Illinois and going back again an honest one!" In a letter to a friend, he admitted that he had made himself "the most detested man who ever sat in Congress, enveloped by a crowd who long and pray for a chance to extirpate me."

Returning to the *Tribune,* he continued to make powerful enemies with his fearless crusades. Businessmen were furious when he blamed them for provoking strikes by refusing to bargain with their employees—a view that became the Wagner National Labor Relations Act eighty years later. They were indignant when, in 1851, he hired a Socialist economist as the *Tribune's* London correspondent—Karl Marx.

By 1854 New York City officials were up in arms over his attacks on them for dirty streets and insufficient parks. Steamship lines were furious at his demands that they stop shipping immigrants like cattle. The armed forces were enraged when he urged "abolishing the Army, which is an absurd nuisance, unworthy of the nineteenth century; reducing the Navy to six frigates and a few sloops; and cutting down all salaries to what the work is worth." Southerners offended by his abolitionist views canceled their subscriptions.

Unpredictable, uncontrollable, unpopular in high places, Greeley was rebuffed when he sought the support of Weed and Seward for nomination as the Whig candidate in the 1854 gubernatorial election. He was humiliated when, instead, they put up for Lieutenant Governor his arch foe and bitter rival, Henry Raymond of the *Times.* He never forgave them.

In 1856 he helped wreck the Whig Party by joining in organizing the Republican Party. Although he supported Douglas in the famous Lincoln-Douglas debates of 1858, the nationwide publicity he gave the debates helped lift Lincoln to national eminence as a bright star in the Republican sky.

Another uproar broke over Greeley's head in 1859 when, after John Brown's raid on Harpers Ferry, it was revealed that Greeley had contributed seven hundred dollars to Brown's movement.

The Democratic press cried that Greeley ought to hang beside Brown. The *Tribune* replied defiantly, "When American Slavery shall have passed away, mankind universally will hail John Brown as a martyr." The *Tribune* became so unpopular down South that its reporters had to disguise themselves.

At the Republican Convention in Chicago in 1860, Boss Weed worked like a demon trying to win the Presidential nomination for Seward, bribing many delegates. But at a crucial moment in the balloting, Greeley swung thirty-six votes over to Abraham Lincoln and won him the nomination instead.

When Lincoln took office, he often turned to Greeley for *Tribune* approval of his policies. But the editor was frequently impatient with the President's caution in prosecuting the war against the Confederacy. Sometimes Greeley pleaded with Lincoln; sometimes he tried to bully him; sometimes he goaded him with scorn. The President kept a special pigeonhole in his desk exclusively for Greeley's letters.

Worried over the *Tribune's* fretting on Northern morale, Lincoln tried to keep Greeley's support by writing letters designed to be shown to him. One said, "I need not tell you that I have the highest confidence in Mr. Greeley. He is a great power. Having him firmly behind me will be as helpful to me as an army of 100,000 men. . . . He and I should stand together, and let no minor differences come between us."

Greeley kept prodding Lincoln to issue a proclamation ending slavery in the United States. The President replied, "My paramount object is to save the Union, and not either to save or destroy slavery." But public opinion overwhelmingly supported Greeley, and Lincoln reluctantly issued the Emancipation Proclamation.

When the Civil War dragged on through the summer of 1864, Greeley grew discouraged and horrified at the bloodshed. On his own he sought to arrange a peace conference between North and South, going to Canada to meet with two Southerners who professed to be "peace emissaries" from Jefferson Davis. Lincoln was highly skeptical, but let Greeley meet them for unofficial exploratory talks. Then Lincoln pulled the rug out from under Greeley by sending his secretary, John Jay, to join them and bluntly state the President's minimum terms for peace.

This move gave the Southerners the excuse they were looking for to explode a propaganda bomb, breaking off negotiations and charging the North with prolonging the war by making unreasonable demands. Lincoln had known this was their plan, and shrewdly let Greeley take the blame. An avalanche of denunciation fell upon the unhappy editor's head for "meddling and bungling" and "cuddling with traitors."

Furious, Greeley opposed Lincoln's reelection, even when a mutual friend reported the President had said, "I have been a lifelong admirer of Greeley. I consider him the ablest editor in the United States, if not the world, and I believe he exerts more influence in the country than any other man, not excepting the President. He is the equal, if not the superior, of Benjamin Franklin." This flattery softened Greeley, but it was only his agonized conclusion that the nation needed Lincoln that finally led the editor to urge his countrymen to keep the President in office. They did.

"I've changed my mind for the country's sake—*not his!*" Greeley snapped. Lincoln smiled, "I don't suppose I have any right to complain. Uncle Horace agrees with me pretty often, after all. I reckon he's with us four days out of seven."

When the war was over, Greeley staunchly supported Lincoln's plea of generosity toward the defeated South. When Lincoln was assassinated, Jefferson Davis was captured, jailed in irons, and exhibited to visitors like a captive tiger. He was held without trial for two years. Greeley indignantly joined other Northerners in signing a bond to free him until a trial was held. Nothing he had ever done in his career made him more unpopular with Americans of the North.

"At last a man has turned up who is more unpopular than Jeff Davis, and that is Horace Greeley," John Bigelow, wealthy publisher of the *Evening Post,* observed. "I think if Greeley could be hung now, the country would be content to let Jeff run!" Greeley defied the uproar, declaring, "So long as any man was seeking to overthrow our government, he was my enemy. From the hour in which he laid down his arms, he was my *formerly* erring countryman!"

His old political fever began to manifest itself again in 1872, when he became disenchanted with the corruption of the Republican administration of President Grant. He was encouraged by a dinner celebrating his sixty-first birthday, at which speakers like Mark Twain, Bret Harte, and P. T. Barnum declared, "In Mr. Greeley, the average American sees himself magnified." That year he opposed Grant's reelection, running as Presidential candidate of the Republican Liberal faction. The unexpected endorsement of the Democratic Party, however, proved the kiss of death among Northern voters. He lost badly.

This lampoon of Greeley and the *Tribune* predicted Greeley's defeat in 1872.

"I'm the worst-beaten man that ever ran for high office," he sighed to his two daughters. "And I have been assailed so bitterly that I hardly know whether I was running for the Presidency or the penitentiary!"

Soon afterward, crushed by the death of his wife and the strain of a lifetime of public crusading, he suffered a breakdown. Pathetically confused, he wrote a dozen versions of a will beginning, "I, Horace Greeley, finding myself bankrupt, without hope, ruinously tempted by the glittering bait of the Presidency . . ." He died on November 29, 1872.

At his funeral forty thousand New Yorkers and great figures from all over the nation turned out to honor the man who had pinched, stung, scolded, and lambasted his fellow Americans, driving them forward to a fairer and better society. He would always be their Uncle Horace, the irascible, cussed old coot who made them think, whether they wanted to or not; who defied unpopularity because he loved them more than the opportunists who did not dare to tell them the truth.

Many of the public welfare features enjoyed by Americans today were first advocated in one form or another by Horace Greeley—exposure of fraudulent patent medicines; the right of men to jobs; abolition of capital punishment; Social Security; unemployment insurance; Medicare; profit sharing; women's suffrage; regional development; government anti-smoking measures; city parks; child labor laws; minimum wage law.

Above all, he will be remembered as the conscience of a President—the exasperating American whose unquenchable eloquence helped free the slaves and restore the Union.

7

"I Was Not Born To Be Forced"

Henry David Thoreau

In 1907 Mahatma Gandhi, seeking a way to overthrow British rule in India without an army, came across a pamphlet called *Civil Disobedience.* Its American author, writing half a century earlier, had a solution for him. Defeat the law when it is tyrannical, advised the writer, by organizing mass disobedience and filling the jails. Gandhi's campaign of civil disobedience won Indian independence thirty years later.

In the 1960s Gandhi's example inspired an American Negro leader, Dr. Martin Luther King Jr., to imitate the same techniques of non-violent passive resistance. By leading Americans, both black and white, in disobeying local anti-Negro statutes to protest their illegality under the Constitution, King set in motion a new civil rights movement in America.

The author of *Civil Disobedience,* the powerful tract that inspired both Gandhi and King, was one of the most stubborn individualists in American history. Henry David Thoreau was born in Concord, Massachusetts, on July 12, 1817. A short, solidly built youth with unsmiling mouth and piercing blue eyes, he won a scholarship to Harvard when he was only sixteen.

His first act of defiance was to attend chapel in a green home-spun coat instead of a black one as required. He annoyed his professors by indifference to their opinions and his classmates by coldness toward their company. Although he was brilliant, he disdained to make any effort to stand at the top of his class.

After graduating in 1837, he taught school in Concord for a while, but quit when he was ordered to discipline his pupils by flogging them. He experimented in his father's small pencil-making shop until he had developed a pencil equal in quality to the best London imports. Then he left.

"Why should I make another pencil?" he shrugged. "I would not do again what I have done once." He refused to enter busi-ness. "Trade curses everything it handles," he declared. "And though you trade in messages from Heaven, the whole curse of trade attaches to the business."

He had a more valuable way to use his time, he told his father—walking around the countryside of Concord to study it and reflect. In this decision he had been strongly influenced by Ralph Waldo Emerson's book *Nature,* which urged turning away from society to contemplate nature in solitude and tune one's spirit to the infinite. Thoreau soon knew the fields, forests, and streams around his hometown as well as a fox or a bird, absorb-ing himself in observations of leaves, flowers, acorns, and the nests of birds and fish.

Some neighbors considered him eccentric; others saw him as an irresponsible loafer. Their opinions left him unruffled. He had written in his last year at Harvard, "The fear of displeasing the world ought not in the least to influence my actions." And it never did.

Deciding to make living itself his occupation, he supported his interests by brief bouts of manual labor whenever he needed money—building a boat or fence, planting, grafting, or survey-ing. He needed very little cash because he kept his needs lim-ited in order to give himself as much free time as possible. "If I should sell both my forenoons and afternoons to society, as most appear to do," he wrote, "I am sure that for me there would be nothing left worth living for." This same philosophy strongly influences many of today's hippies and flower children.

Working as a land surveyor appealed to him most because of his love of hiking and making scientific measurements of trees, ponds, and mountains. He was said to be able to follow a wood path at night by his feet alone, and to estimate heights and distances accurately by eye.

Enjoying solitude, he felt that he missed little by avoiding the company of most people. "The mass never comes up to the standard of its best member," he once wrote, "but on the contrary degrades itself to the level with the lowest."

One of the few close friends he made was Ralph Waldo Emerson, who had moved to Concord with his family. Theirs was a teacher-pupil relationship. Emerson, fourteen years older, strongly influenced the writing style and speech of his young admirer. He taught Thoreau not to accept any ideas second-hand, but to depend upon original thinking.

Emerson was often irked, however, when Thoreau took to disputing *his* ideas. "His first instinct on hearing a proposition," Emerson wrote of his disciple, "was to controvert it, so impatient was he of the limitations of our daily thought. This habit, of course, is a little chilling to the social affections." Emerson nevertheless let Thoreau board with his family in exchange for doing some odd jobs as a handyman.

Thoreau was also allowed to join the company of Emerson's celebrated friends, including Nathaniel Hawthorne, Henry James, and Horace Greeley. But he soon found even so brilliant a circle no substitute for solitude and his own reflections.

In the summer of 1845 he decided to try living apart from society. He cleared some acreage for Emerson, who gave him permission to build a cabin that cost him $28.12 two miles away on the wooded shores of Walden Pond.

"I went to the woods because I wished to live deliberately," he wrote later in *Walden*, "to front only the essential facts of life, and see if I could not learn what it had to teach, and not, when I came to die, discover that I had not lived." So for two years he lived beside the pond's green, still waters, leading a self-reliant existence of contemplation and hard work. He baked his own bread, raised garden vegetables, fished, and trapped wild game.

Needing little else, he relished living as earliest man might have lived, close to nature, in communion with bird, beast, and plant. He made a pet of a mouse, and noted of a scarlet tanager that it flew through the green foliage "as if it would ignite the leaves." He observed in *Walden*, "Most of the luxuries and many of the so-called comforts of life are not only dispensable, but positive hindrances to the elevation of mankind."

His hermit's existence deepened his crustiness with others. One acquaintance sighed, "I love Henry but I cannot like him. And as for taking his arm, I should as soon think of taking the arm of an elm tree!" Thoreau's popularity was not increased by his open contempt for the preoccupation of most men with goals of money, prestige, and status.

"The greater part of what my neighbors call good," he wrote in *Walden*, "I believe in my soul to be bad. . . . If a man does not keep pace with his companions, perhaps it is because he hears a different drummer." Today's hippies phrase it differently when they say, "We're opting out of the rat race," but they mean the same thing Thoreau meant.

He published two books during his lifetime—*A Week on the Concord and Merrimack Rivers* in 1849 and *Walden* in 1854. Both were dismal failures, but *Walden* was later recognized as a great and original classic of lyric naturalism.

Like most New Englanders Thoreau opposed slavery, but he went further by refusing to respect it as the law of the land. He wrote, "Those who, while they disapprove of the character

Thoreau's house at Walden is featured on the title page of the book.

and measures of a government, yield to it their allegiance and support are undoubtedly its most conscientious supporters, and so frequently the most serious obstacles to reform." When the United States declared war on Mexico on May 13, 1846, he denounced the action, like Lincoln and Greeley, as an imperialist adventure to expand slave territory.

Thoreau resisted the only way he could—by refusing to pay his Massachusetts poll tax. The government was not going to get a cent of *his* to support a war he abhorred!

"I have heard some of my townsmen say, 'I should like to have them order me out to help put down an insurrection of the slaves, or to march to Mexico—see if I would go'; and yet these very men have each . . . by their money, furnished a substitute. The soldier is applauded who refuses to serve in an unjust war by those who do not refuse to sustain the unjust government which makes the war."

Thoreau's example was followed a century later when folk singer Joan Baez refused to pay that portion of her income tax which would be spent by the government in armaments and prosecution of the Vietnam War.

Threatened with jail, Thoreau stubbornly persisted in his refusal to pay his tax. "I was not born to be forced," he said firmly. So he was imprisoned in the Concord jail behind two-foot-thick walls.

"The walls," he wrote, "seemed a great waste of stone and mortar. . . . They locked the door on my meditations, which followed them out again without let or hindrance, and *they* were all that was dangerous. As they could not reach me, they had resolved to punish my body. . . . I saw that the State was half-witted . . . that it did not know its friends from its foes, and I lost all my remaining respect for it, and pitied it." That night, lying in prison, he listened to the town clock strike and the evening sounds of the village.

Musing ironically, it seemed to him that he was in a Rhine village of the Middle Ages, and that the voices he heard outside his cell belonged to knights and burghers.

"I saw to what extent the people among whom I lived could be trusted as good neighbors and friends; that their friendship was for summer weather only; that they did not greatly purpose to do right; that they were a distinct race from me by their prejudices and superstitions."

He added caustically, "In their sacrifices to humanity, they ran no risks, not even to their property."

Hearing that Thoreau had been jailed, Emerson hurried to the prison. "What are you doing in there, Henry?" he demanded in dismay. Thoreau fixed him with a sardonic glance.

"What are you doing out there, Waldo?" he replied.

In the morning he was angry to learn that he was free. Someone had paid his tax for him, probably his aunt, Maria Thoreau. "I'll be back again next year," he told the jailer. "I will never pay tax to any government for an unjust cause." Then he continued calmly about the business that had originally brought him to town—getting a shoe mended before leading a berrying party into the hills.

In 1849 he wrote the famous tract *Civil Disobedience,* portraying the State as a malevolent institution that threatened the liberty of the individual. While he had been in jail, he related, "I felt as if I alone of all my townsmen had paid my tax." The real tax one owed, Thoreau felt, was self-sacrifice in the cause of personal freedom.

He called for civil disobedience against unjust acts by unjust governments. "We should be men first and subjects afterward," he declared. "It is not desirable to cultivate a respect for the law, so much as for the right." Americans, he insisted, must cease to hold slaves and make war on poor Mexicans, "though it cost them their existence as a people."

He did not feel obligated to give up his own interests to crusade on behalf of the oppressed. But—"I must first see, at least, that I do not pursue them sitting upon another man's shoulders.

I must get off him first, that he may pursue his contemplations too."

He blamed his fellow citizens for tolerating unjust laws until a majority got around to changing them: "It is the fault of the government itself that the remedy is worse than the evil." Why was the government not intelligent enough, instead, to heed the voices of reform? "Why does it not cherish its wise minority? . . . Why does it always crucify Christ, and excommunicate Copernicus and Luther, and pronounce Washington and Franklin rebels?"

A citizen was justified, Thoreau insisted, in rebelling against law and refusing to bow to the will of the majority when he was convinced he was right. "If the injustice . . . is of such a nature that it requires you to be the agent of injustice to another, then, I say, break the law. Let your life be a counter-friction to stop the machine. . . . As for adopting the ways the State has provided for remedying the evil, I know not of such ways. They take too much time, and a man's life will be gone."

He called upon abolitionists to withdraw all support from the government of Massachusetts immediately, and not wait until they had a majority of one before they ended slavery. "It is enough if they have God on their side, without waiting for that other one. Moreover, any man with more right than his neighbors constitutes a majority of one already."

A minority was powerless, Thoreau believed, only so long as it supported the majority. "It is irresistible when it clogs by its whole weight. If the alternative is to keep all just men in prison, or give up war and slavery, the State will not hesitate which to choose. . . . This is, in fact, the definition of a peaceful revolution."

Thoreau's eloquent advocacy of passive resistance to unjust laws was a stick of dynamite with a delayed-action fuse. *Civil Disobedience* inspired protest movements not only in America but all over the world. It is still setting off explosions in our own nation, especially in Negro slums.

Henry David Thoreau.

Thoreau did not believe in violent opposition, but was aware that it might follow when the government failed to heed the voices of protest. "Suppose blood should flow," he wrote. "Is there not a sort of blood shed when the conscience is wounded? Through this wound a man's real manhood and immortality flow out, and he bleeds to an everlasting death. I see this blood flowing now."

For the rest of his life Thoreau lived by his stubborn principles. He left Concord only to lecture occasionally, but mostly to take nature walks through other countrysides. Lodging cheaply with farmers and fishermen, he would avoid roads for the fields, climbing trees for bird and squirrel nests, wading into pools for water plants. He deplored settled areas where the ax had brought civilization.

"Thank God," he sighed, "they cannot cut down the clouds!"

Toward the end of his life Thoreau became an active abolitionist, helping fugitive slaves escape to Canada. In 1857, like Greeley, he met and supported John Brown, the controversial Kansas leader of anti-slave raids. When Brown was captured trying to foment a slave insurrection, Thoreau wrote that even if he was something of a lunatic reformer, he was at least an idealistic lunatic who acted on his principles.

Thoreau gave notice that he would speak in Brown's defense at the Town Hall. Concord's selectmen warned that he would outrage public opinion if he did, and they refused to ring the Hall's bell to signal his speech. Thoreau rang it himself. Faced with a hostile audience, he justified Brown's violence as the consequence of the refusal of American society to heed the civil disobedience of the abolitionists.

"I hear many condemn these men because they were so few," he cried. "When were the good and the brave ever in the majority? . . . Is it not possible that an individual may be right and a government wrong? Are laws to be enforced simply because they are made? Or declared by any number of men to be good, if they are *not* good?"

His eloquence swayed minds and changed hearts, winning stormy applause. He was begged to repeat his speech in leading cities of Massachusetts. Important papers like Greeley's *Tribune* reported it to the nation. Widespread support grew for clemency to be shown John Brown. When Virginia hung him anyhow, Thoreau sighed, "So we defend ourselves."

On May 6, 1862, at the tragically young age of forty-five, Thoreau died in Concord of tuberculosis. He left behind few worldly goods but a rich heritage of rugged individualism. "A man is rich," he had written, "in proportion to the number of things he can afford to let alone." The townspeople of Concord, who had begun by scorning him as an eccentric dropout from society, ended by admiring and respecting him as one of the most original and courageous thinkers America had ever produced. No learned society ever honored him by an office, no college ever offered him a chair on its faculty, but it was Thoreau who set great world forces in motion by influencing such important movers and shakers of their time as Mahatma Gandhi and Martin Luther King.

Ironically, it was his old friend Emerson who suggested that Thoreau may have wasted his life tragically on small things by refusing to join society: "I cannot help counting it a fault in him that he had no ambition. Wanting this, instead of engineering for all America, he was the captain of a huckleberry party." But this was to miss the whole thrust of Thoreau's conviction—that those who involved themselves with the goals of ambition were wasting *their* lives.

Right or wrong, he anticipated many hippies of the 1960s who dropped out of American society, rejecting the Establishment to search for inner experience and personal freedom.

Thoreau, who declared, "I never found the companion that was so companionable as solitude," spoke to today's Americans anxious to escape crowded cities and suburbs. Searching for isolated lakes and streams, camping out in the nation's parks and forests, they too seek Walden-like solitude.

Thoreau was also the spiritual father of both the civil rights movement and anti-Vietnam War protests. Their supporters believed with him, "The law will never make men free; it is men who have got to make the law free. They are the lovers of law and order who observe the law when the government breaks it."

But perhaps nothing Thoreau wrote ever reflected the significance of his own life to Americans more than these words: "All this worldly wisdom was once the unamiable heresy of some wise man." There was no better epitaph for the rugged individualist and thorny non-conformist who persistently marched to the sound of a different drummer.

8

The Branded Hand

Jonathan Walker

They dragged him into the street from the courthouse, the irons around his legs clanking on the paving stones. A living skeleton after four months of near-starvation in a Pensacola dungeon, he was forced into a public pillory.

Jeering townspeople, faces full of hate, hands and pockets full of missiles to express their contempt, pelted him with rotten eggs, stable ordure, and bags of filth.

"Rotten Yankee slave stealer!"

When the mob had had its fill of reviling him, Jonathan Walker was unlocked from the pillory and dragged back to the courthouse. A burly marshal stood waiting, legs apart, in front of a blazing fire in an iron brazier. The prisoner was thrown at his feet, so soiled and smeared that the marshal's nostrils twitched in revulsion. He gave sharp orders that could barely be heard above the roar of the excited crowd rushing for seats in the crowded courtroom.

A court officer pressed Jonathan Walker to his knees. Raising the prisoner's right hand, he began tying it palm upward to a railing. Walker whispered, "There is no need to tie my hand—I will hold it steady." He was ignored.

The marshal checked the hot branding iron in the fire. Turning it in the flames another moment or two, he lifted it out. The crowd sighed in rapture as it caught sight of the blackened letters of the brand—"SS" for "Slave Stealer."

The marshal held it aloft like the eagle standard that once led Roman centurions into battle against their enemies. Then he pressed it firmly against the ball of the prisoner's hand, holding it there for twenty seconds. It made a spattering noise like a handful of salt in the fire as the skin seared and gave way to the hot iron. Walker convulsed.

The crowd roared approval as he was dragged back to his dungeon. For nine of the next eleven months he remained in irons. Lying in the filthy, dark cell, his whole universe black and still, Jonathan Walker had no way of knowing that the terrible brand on his hand had seared more than his flesh alone. It was also searing the souls of millions of Americans in the North, enraging them into a storm of fury against the slave-owning South.

He was born in Massachusetts in the early nineteenth century. For some years he studied the trade of boatbuilding in the shipyards of East Harwich. Shipping out on coastal vessels, he learned enough seamanship to become a skipper of a small ship of his own.

Like most New Englanders of his day, Jonathan Walker believed slavery was immoral.

Like most New Englanders of his day, he shared the moral conviction that slavery was wrong. In 1843, he was delighted when neighboring Vermont passed an act designed to thwart the Fugitive Slave Act of Congress. That same year the second Seminole Indian War ended in Florida, with the Indians nearly exterminated. White Floridians, eager to open up their territory and seek statehood, began building railroads to link their settlements. Captain Walker was offered a contract to bring construction materials down from the North and supervise building the railroad section out from Pensacola.

In the spring of 1844, economic necessity led him to sail to Florida with the required cargo and undertake the job. His employers provided him with slave labor, whom he treated as kindly as possible, but over whose living conditions he had no control. His indignation over their treatment was not lost on the slaves, who knew him to be their friend.

One night three slaves came to him in secret, begging him to help them escape by boat to the British Bahamas, where slavery had been abolished. Under British law, the moment they touched Bahamian soil they would be free men. Walker knew the grave risk he would be running, but his New England conscience would not let him say no to three human beings pleading for the freedom he believed to be every man's right. The Lord, he felt, had chosen him to be their savior.

"I'll do it," he told them. On the night of June 22, 1844, Walker and the three slaves prepared to slip away under cover of darkness from Pensacola in an open boat. At the very last moment they were joined by four other desperate slaves who had heard of the escape and begged to be allowed to go along. Walker waved them into the boat.

For several weeks they alternately rowed and sailed southeast through the seemingly endless Gulf of Mexico, planning to slip through the Florida Keys, sail around the straits of Florida, and head for Grand Bahama Island. Week after week they fought violent summer squalls and equatorial heat on meager food and water rations that grew perilously low.

Ill with sunstroke, Walker was delirious for long periods. "My strength and flesh were nearly gone," he wrote later. But he persisted in sailing on and by July 8 had managed to take his contraband cargo over seven hundred miles toward freedom.

On that day the open boat with its one white man and seven Negroes was spotted by two government sloops off the Florida Keys. Bearing down swiftly, they overtook and captured the boat, taking its occupants to Key West.

Here Walker was placed in double irons and sent back to Pensacola for punishment as a slave stealer. Thrown into a dungeon, he was chained to the wall—"secured in my cage like some rabid, dangerous animal," he related afterward. By the time he was brought to trial months later, his leg irons had dug into his flesh. Shriveled from untreated illness and virtual starvation, he was so thin that his bones "were covered with little more than the skin wrapped around them." Neither the judge nor jury he faced in Pensacola was outraged or moved to pity by his condition.

On November 11, 1844, the jury found him guilty of slave stealing. The judge sentenced him to stand in the public pillory; to be branded on the hand with the letters "SS"; to pay a fine; to serve a jail term for each of the seven slaves he had abducted; to pay all costs of his prosecution; and to be held in jail until every cent of his fines was paid.

When news of the branding of Jonathan Walker reached the North, New England erupted in widespread indignation. Abolitionist leaders in Boston began raising funds to free him from the Pensacola jail. But it was not until 1848 that enough money had been collected to let them negotiate with the Florida courts for the release of the celebrated prisoner.

He left Florida with Southern boos, jeers, and shouts of hatred ringing in his ears. He arrived in Boston to receive a hero's welcome at one uproarious reception after another. Jonathan Walker was the most genuine martyr the abolitionists of New England had ever had, and they made the most of him.

He was taken to meet the region's poet laureate, tall, swarthy John Greenleaf Whittier, a fervent Quaker abolitionist. Whittier quickly saw in the stigmata on Jonathan Walker's hand the same significance as the bleeding nail marks on the hands of another martyr on Calvary centuries before. Walker's branded hand, Whittier felt, was a sign of God prophesying the deliverance of the slaves of America.

After their meeting he wrote what was to be his most impassioned poem, a celebration of Jonathan Walker's heroism—*The Branded Hand*. Its moving, effective verses stirred Northern emotions against slavery as nothing else had been able to do before then. Composer George W. Clark set the incendiary words to music and sang them himself at anti-slavery meetings throughout New England. Few verses were recited or sung more often in homes and schools, right up to the Civil War. Two of the most famous verses were these:

> *Then lift that manly right-hand, bold ploughman of the wave!*
> *Its branded palm shall prophesy, "SALVATION TO THE SLAVE!"*
> *Hold up its fire-wrought language, that who reads may feel*
> *His heart swell strong within him, his sinews change to steel.*

> *Welcome home again, brave seaman! With thy thoughtful brow and grey,*
> *And the old heroic spirit of our earlier, better day,*
> *With that front of calm endurance, on whose steady nerve in vain*
> *Pressed the iron of the prison, smote the fiery shafts of pain!*

Jonathan Walker was lionized by Boston abolitionists who made him tell his story over and over again to fresh audiences. Northerners gasped as he held up his branded hand to let them see the brutality of a slave-owning society.

In Providence, Rhode Island, a tremendous reception for Walker was attended by Owen Lovejoy, brother of the martyred abolitionist editor Elijah Lovejoy, who had been shot and killed in Illinois by pro-slavery mobs. Three thousand people jammed the seats, aisles, and doorways to hear Walker describe his experiences and show his branded hand.

He appeared at other rallies throughout the North, moving thousands of shocked Americans to join the ranks of the abolitionists. The thundering guns of Fort Sumter found an aroused North determined that slavery must be ended.

When Lincoln signed the Emancipation Proclamation in 1862, abolitionists knew that three invisible hands had signed the historic bill before him—first, the branded hand of Jonathan Walker; second, the gifted hand of John Greenleaf Whittier; finally, the hammering hand of Horace Greeley.

The white Freedom Riders of the 1960s, who went South to free Negroes from a century of post-Civil War oppression, were acting in the best tradition of Jonathan Walker. Instead of martyrdom by pillory, prison, and a branded hand, civil rights workers Michael Schwerner, Andrew Goodman, and James E. Chaney were murdered in Mississippi in June 1964.

When the state failed to convict any of their murderers, a federal court jury found seven men guilty of "conspiracy to violate the civil rights" of the dead men, and they were given jail terms.

But the murderers have yet to be convicted of murder.

9

"If the Women Mean to Wear the Pants"

Amelia Jenks Bloomer

Gasps rose above the streets of the thriving little mill town of Seneca Falls, New York. Heads snapped around. Men's eyes popped open in disbelief. Women's mouths fell open in outrage. Ministers went rigid with rage and horror.

"Hussy!" hissed one hoop-skirted dowager.

Mrs. Amelia Jenks Bloomer swept down the street with majestic poise, pointedly ignoring the furor in her wake. She was a petite, dainty woman of five feet four, weighing only a hundred pounds, with bold blue eyes and dark red hair, and she fully enjoyed the commotion she was creating.

It was more than time, she felt, that people began noticing women as individuals with minds and wills of their own. They had been kept invisible, second-class citizens long enough, forced to live in the shadows of men. Why *should* women dress and behave as demurely as men expected "respectable" women to dress and behave?

The cause of the uproar that morning in Seneca Falls was the costume she was wearing. Instead of the modest, all-concealing hoopskirt, her attire seemed to have shrunk her hoopskirt up alarmingly to her knees. The lower half of her legs were revealed as clad in full Turkish trousers gathered at her ankles. It was as if Amelia Bloomer were calling the world's attention to the shocking fact that beneath their voluminous hoopskirts, women had two separate legs—like men!—and not wheels or rollers on which they glided.

Her picture in this "brazen" new costume was soon reproduced in newspapers all over the country, astonishing incredulous Americans. The *New York Times* of September 18, 1851, reported the emergence of the "Bloomer costume" in New York City on the front page. Two daring "Bloomers" had appeared on Broadway, two on Washington Square, one on Sixth Avenue.

"A crowd of 'conservatives,'" noted the *Times*, "manifested their hostility to this progressive movement by derision."

All around the nation women expressed outrage, men hooted in mockery, at the revolt of Amelia Jenks Bloomer against the confinement of hoopskirts. Yet it was largely her courage to continue wearing bloomers that helped sound the death knell of the hoopskirts that had grown so wide as to make it difficult for women to get in and out of doorways. By the 1860s, hoops were on their way out, and more practical fashions were on their way in.

Bloomers marked the beginning of a revolution in women's dress that still reverberates in today's styles.

She was born Amelia Jenks in a small town in Cortland County, New York, in 1818. Her parents were strict, hardworking, abstinent Presbyterians. She had only a few years of formal education at the local district school, but became an avid reader, greatly stimulated by deep thinkers of the day.

At seventeen she taught school for a while. Her questing mind and an eagerness to meet intellectuals, however, led her to take a job as governess with a wealthy family of Waterloo in Seneca County. Here she met Dexter C. Bloomer, a young Quaker law student, and found that they shared the same "advanced" ideas of the day, with a common scorn of convention and conformism. They were married in April 1840.

It told a good deal about both Amelia Jenks Bloomer and her husband that she had no difficulty in persuading him to eliminate the word "obey" from their wedding ceremony. She also refused a glass of wine at their wedding reception because she was a dedicated teetotaler like her parents, convinced that drinking was the curse of America.

She was scarcely alone in her opinion. French visitor Gustave de Beaumont, traveling with his friend Tocqueville, observed of early nineteenth-century Americans, "They have but a single fault, which is that of drinking too much." Anti-liquor groups were springing up on all sides, including the Sons of Temperance, the Good Templars, and the Female Abstinence Society. They fanned out over the nation, pleading with alcoholics to reform and "sign the pledge." Amelia Jenks Bloomer also became a dedicated temperance crusader.

She and Dexter moved to Seneca Falls, New York, where, with a partner, he published and edited the *Seneca City Courier*. Amelia wrote columns on the moral problems of the day, especially alcoholism. Joining the Seneca Falls Ladies' Temperance Society, she was soon made its vice-president.

Her closest friend was a leading suffragette of the day, Mrs. Elizabeth Cady Stanton, who issued a call in 1848 for the first Women's Rights Convention. It was held right in Seneca Falls, at the Wesleyan Chapel, and Amelia attended. Covering it for the *Courier*, she listened to the suffragettes demand not only the vote, but justice for the American wife, because "man has made her, if married, civilly dead." Wives, they insisted, should have full equality with their husbands before the law in every respect.

"If the women mean to wear the pants," editor James Gordon Bennett mocked them in his New York *Herald*, "then they must also be ready in case of war to buckle on the sword!"

Despite her friendship and admiration for Mrs. Stanton, Amelia did not sign the convention's "Declaration of Independence for Women." She was not, at that time, a fully convinced feminist. Her interest was primarily in temperance.

When the Seneca Falls Ladies' Temperance Society decided to publish a temperance magazine to be called *The Lily*, they asked Amelia to undertake it for them. So she became editor of the first women's magazine in America. *The Lily* was an instant success because Amelia shrewdly featured all news of suicides, murders, and terrible accidents that could be attributed to drinking. It was effective propaganda.

Wives were warned against letting children "inherit the vices of their drunken, tobacco-chewing fathers," and against serving liquor on New Year's Eve or flavoring mince pies.

But under the influence of Mrs. Stanton, Amelia began to take up more and more feminist causes—arguing the case for easier divorce laws for unsuitable marriages; for better schools; and above all for woman suffrage in local, state, and national elections. *The Lily's* circulation soared steadily.

When her husband's paper supported the successful candidacy of William Henry Harrison in Greeley's "Tippecanoe and Tyler, Too," campaign, Dexter Bloomer was rewarded by being named postmaster of Seneca Falls, and Amelia became "deputy postmaster." She turned her room at the post office into an informal women's club for Seneca Falls' crusaders for feminism and temperance, most of whom were her friends.

One day Mrs. Stanton brought along a visiting relative—Mrs. Elizabeth Smith Miller, fashionable daughter of wealthy abolitionist Gerrit Smith. Mrs. Miller's costume fascinated Amelia, who described it as "a skirt that came a little below the knee, and trowsers of the same material—black satin." Amelia had never seen anything like it.

"My father designed it," Mrs. Miller explained. "It's wonderful for the long walks I like to take in the countryside around West Centre, New York, where I live. It's so comfortable and convenient, I wear it all the time now."

"It would be wonderful here, too," Amelia glowed, "what with all the mud in our streets after a rain!"

When Mrs. Miller went home to West Centre, Amelia Bloomer made a similar costume for herself and began to shock Seneca Falls by wearing it everywhere in the town. Scandalized or amused local citizens began to refer to the costume as Amelia's "bloomers," a term that soon became used loosely to describe any form of women's divided skirts, knickerbockers, or underpants.

Delighting in the sensation she was causing, Amelia found her new attire not only lighter and eye-catching, but also spiritually uplifting. She had never felt so free and unconstrained, and took pleasure in her more natural, liberated movements. She began to see the possibilities of the new costume as a step to free women physically and spiritually from the cumbersome hoopskirt. Bloomers could become a national symbol of feminine emancipation.

In 1850 she began crusading for women's dress reform in *The Lily,* urging the universal wearing of bloomers. Her campaign provoked a nationwide controversy, with bloomers more hotly argued over than the slavery issue. Jenny Lind, the "Swedish Nightingale" brought to America for concerts by P. T. Barnum, won enormous publicity by permitting daguerreotypes of herself in bloomers. Bloomers as a new style even swept across the Atlantic to agitate the English.

"I am vastly amused by the Bloomer discussion," the Duke of Wellington wrote to Lady Salisbury in 1850. "It is impossible that the Costume should be adopted."

In 1851, when Mrs. Stanton called a third Women's Rights Convention in Syracuse, New York, she appeared on the speakers' platform in bloomers. So did suffragettes Susan B. Anthony, Lucy Stone, and other delegates. Mrs. Stanton argued that bloomers would let women enter more male occupations, in which hoopskirts would hamper them. As for raising male eyebrows by a display of female limbs, Mrs. Stanton insisted—somewhat

ONE OF THE DELIGHTFUL RESULTS OF BLOOMERISM.—THE LADIES WILL POP THE QUESTION.

Superior Creature. "SAY! OH, SAY, DEAREST! WILL YOU BE MINE?" &c., &c.

A cartoon from *Punch*, deriding Mrs. Bloomer's fashion.

unconvincingly—that the wearing of bloomers would decrease emphasis on feminine sexual characteristics: ". . . and so we shall all lead far purer and higher lives!"

To their dismay, however, the feminists found the public was far more excited over their bloomers than their ideas. Amelia Bloomer herself did not share their chagrin. She loved being in the eye of the storm and enjoyed being in great demand as a lecturer—with the understanding that she would, of course, appear on the platform in her famous costume.

A wealthy soft drink manufacturer named Townsend, who had a vested interest in turning people away from liquor to sarsaparilla, paid the expenses of Amelia, Susan Anthony, and the Reverend Antoinette Brown to deliver temperance lectures in New York City and all around New York State.

The biggest audiences were drawn by Amelia, whose bloomers created a bigger stir than anything she had to say about a woman's right to divorce a drunken husband.

But most feminists who wore bloomers grew increasingly exasperated by the hoots and howlings of mobs who followed them in the streets. Men whistled and made suggestive remarks. Small boys chanted crude street songs of derision.

"Had I counted the cost of the pantaloon costume," admitted Mrs. Stanton, "I would never have put it on. On, however, I'll never take it off, for now it invokes a principle."

But Antoinette Brown, who had never worn it, advised others "not to become martyrs over a short dress." And Lucy Stone, deciding she had endured enough heckling, abandoned the costume. Mrs. Stanton finally gave up and surrendered her bloomers too. "If Lucy Stone cannot bear the martyrdom of the dress," she sighed, "who, I ask, can?"

By 1853, most of the feminists were out of bloomers except for Amelia Bloomer and the woman who had inspired her to popularize the costume, Mrs. Miller. Although Mrs. Miller had tired of them herself, her father would not let her discard bloomers because he felt that they had become a uniform for an important cause. She also looked well in them.

"Mrs. Miller has a fine figure," admitted Lucy Stone, "and wears the bloomer costume to better advantage than any of the rest of us." One reason for the death of the bloomer fad, undoubtedly, was the preference that women with dumpy figures felt for the concealing full skirt.

Surprisingly, it was among the male sex—which today delights in brief female costumes—that the bloomers were most unpopular. The press was almost unanimous in deriding Amelia Bloomer's fashion, less for aesthetic or moral reasons than for what bloomers symbolized to men.

Men were already irked by feminist demands for equality, the vote, admission into men's jobs, the right to run for office, easier divorce, and anti-liquor laws. They saw the new attire of "the Bloomer girls" as a final act of defiance—rebellion against the male idea of proper female attire. And to most men, women who got out of hoopskirts and into "trowsers" were obviously out to wear the pants in American marriage.

So the feminists dropped the "reform dress," which they felt was costing them more in the loss of public support than the advantages to be gained by persistence in wearing it.

Amelia Jenks Bloomer, her shining hour past and her crusade now an object of merciless mockery, felt that she could no longer abide the jeers of Seneca Falls. She and her husband began to think about Horace Greeley's rousing cry in the *Tribune:* "Go West, young man—and grow up with the country!" So late in 1853 they departed on the Baltimore and Ohio Railroad, which had just pushed to the Ohio border.

Here Dexter bought *The Western Home Visitor* for his wife to edit. When Amelia found the typesetters drinking, she fired them and replaced them with America's first female typesetters, thus grinding two of her axes at once.

In 1855 they moved on west by river steamers. At Saint Joseph, Missouri, Amelia's bloomers were recognized and she was forced ashore to make a speech to thrilled locals. She and Dexter also found a great welcome in Council Bluffs, Iowa, a town that rarely saw any celebrities from the East.

They decided to settle here. Amelia was promptly elected president of the Congregational Church women's club. Dexter opened a law office and prospered. Soon he was elected mayor. Childless until now, Amelia adopted two children and began making homemade jellies that took prizes at county fairs. A late-bloomer in domesticity, she enjoyed it.

She now found bloomers something of a handicap to her, because the high winds of Iowa blew her short skirts up and turned heads even more than her love of attention required. But she persisted in wearing them right up to the sixties, convinced that "dress reform" was still the inevitable wave of the future. Even when she finally returned to long dresses, she continued to wear bloomers around the house as a far more practical costume for cleaning chores.

She remained a crusader for temperance and woman suffrage right up to her death on December 30, 1894. But the crusade for which she will longest be remembered is the one that eventually liberated women to move about as freely and comfortably as men—often more so—in slacks, short skirts, shorts, bikinis, and miniskirts.

10

"The Minority Are Right!"

Eugene Debs

The tall, gangling, bald man of sixty-three faced the hostile jury. In their grim faces he saw the condemnation of an inflamed America at war. He knew they would send him to jail for violating the Espionage Act—for "bringing into contempt, scorn, contumely or disrepute the United States form of government, armed forces, flag or military uniform." The specific charge against him was "interfering with recruiting," because of a fiery address he had made to the Socialist Party Convention in Canton, Ohio, on June 16, 1918.

He had committed the unpardonable sin. Hundreds of thousands of American boys were dying on the battlefields of France. Yet stubborn Eugene Debs had refused to stop branding World War I as an imperialist quarrel between rival capitalist powers over world plunder. It was immoral, he charged, to make workers of the world spill their blood and kill each other to enrich their ruling classes. Worse, it was stupid.

The jury listened coldly to the tall Socialist's efforts to make them understand that he was not a bomb-throwing Bolshevik, but an idealist who peacefully opposed social injustice. "I have never advocated violence in any form," he explained. "I have always believed in education, in intelligence, in enlightenment, and I have always made my appeal to the reason and conscience of the people."

Their hostile eyes told him they were convinced that any dissent in wartime was unpatriotic. Had not the speeches of government and Congressional leaders, reported in newspapers and magazines, made that clear?

"When great changes occur in history," Debs cried, "when great principles are involved, as a rule the majority are wrong. The minority are right!" But on September 14, 1918, he was found guilty and sentenced to ten years in jail.

Neither surprised nor dismayed, Debs welcomed the martyrdom of prison. It would infuriate thousands of American intellectuals, he knew, into becoming Socialists.

He defiantly made it clear that, like Thoreau, he was proud to number himself among the victims of an oppressive society rather than among its supporters. "While there is a lower class, I am in it," he told the court. "While there is a criminal element, I am in it. While there is a soul in prison, I am not free!"

Taken to federal prison in West Virginia, Convict 9653 declared, "I enter the prison doors a flaming revolutionist, my head erect, my spirit untamed, my soul unconquerable!" The iron doors slammed behind him.

Debs was born on November 5, 1855, of immigrant Alsatian parents in Terre Haute, Indiana, a rough frontier railroad town. At fifteen he went to work in railroad shops of the Terre Haute & Indianapolis Railroad, subsequently becoming a locomotive fireman. Reading widely in the social protest literature of that day, he grew indignant over the hardships, long hours, and low wages of railroad men. Five years later he had risen to such labor prominence that he was made Secretary-Treasurer of the national Brotherhood of Firemen, as well as editor of its *Firemen's Magazine*. Working with idealistic zeal, he spent eighteen hours a day building up the union.

But by 1893 he was disillusioned with craft unionism. Only unionizing a whole industry from janitor to dispatcher, he was convinced, could match the strength of capital. Breaking away from the Brotherhood of Firemen, he organized an all-embracing American Railway Union.

A year of severe business panic in 1895 touched off four years of depression. Railroads began firing workers, slashing wages, and lengthening hours. Outraged workers flocked into the ARU. Debs made the Great Northern Railroad his target. When they refused his demand for higher wages, he called out their workers and paralyzed company operations.

Eighteen days later the Great Northern surrendered.

His spectacular success swelled the ranks of the ARU to a membership of 150,000 in just two months.

Now Debs set out to make an example of the Pullman Company, which had just slashed the wages of its workers by as much as 40 percent, while voting its stockholders an 8 percent dividend. Pullman workers were already intensely dissatisfied at being compelled to live in the company town of Pullman, which victimized them by overcharging for rent, gas, and water in company tenements with no bathtubs and only one water faucet for every five families.

"We were born," one worker said bitterly, "in a Pullman house, fed from the Pullman shop, taught in the Pullman school, catechized in the Pullman church, and when we die we shall be buried in the Pullman cemetery and go to the Pullman hell!"

On May 11, the company not only denied workers' demands for wage increases and rent reductions, but fired members of the grievance committee. Three thousand outraged Pullman employees struck. Championing their cause, Debs asked George Pullman to arbitrate. Convinced that a little starvation would bring his "ungrateful" workers to heel, Pullman replied arrogantly, "There is nothing to arbitrate!"

On June 26, the ARU voted to refuse to handle any trains carrying Pullman cars. Directing the strike, Debs urged union solidarity, declaring, "A scab in labor unions is the same as a traitor to his country!" But he also warned workers to maintain tight discipline, refusing to let themselves be provoked into acts of violence or damage to property.

The boycott crippled major railroad operations in twenty-seven states in the Mid- and Far West, virtually paralyzing some lines. Railroad tycoons organized a General Managers' Association, representing twenty-four lines, to crush Debs and the ARU. Strikebreakers were hired, along with *agents provocateurs* to discredit the strikers by setting fire to freight cars in the Chicago yards. Newspapers they controlled obediently screamed that mob rule and insurrection were terrorizing Chicago.

One paper denounced the strike as "a war against the government and against society." Said Debs wryly, "The truth has always been dangerous to the rule of the rogue, the exploiter, the robber. So the truth must be suppressed!"

When public opinion had been sufficiently inflamed, the General Managers signaled United States Attorney General Richard Olney, a former railroad counsel, to obtain a sweeping court injunction against all strike activity for "interfering with the United States mails carried on trains." Olney persuaded

Eugene Debs addressing a crowd.

President Grover Cleveland to order federal troops into Chicago, despite angry protests by Illinois Governor Altgeld.

Defying these moves, Debs refused to call off the strike. Troops moved to man the trains and clear the jammed rail yards. Cavalry charges and infantrymen with fixed bayonets dispersed striking workers. Twenty strikers were killed.

On July 10, Debs and other union leaders were indicted for "conspiracy to obstruct the mails" and refusal to obey the injunction. The strike and the ARU collapsed.

"Both sides," Clarence Darrow declared in court, "recognized that Debs had led a great fight to benefit the toilers and the poor. It was purely a part of the world class struggle, for which no individual can be blamed." But Debs was sentenced to six months in jail. He spent his imprisonment studying Socialist literature and wondering. Had he been wrong in thinking that strong industrial unions could correct the excesses of capitalism? Or, did the whole economic system have to be scrapped by a workers' government?

Released from jail, he was astonished to find over a hundred thousand people waiting at the Chicago railroad station to give him a thunderous ovation. There was growing indignation over a government that threw its weight behind capital to crush labor. Social reformers, clergy, intellectual leaders, and labor spokesmen were demanding anti-trust legislation to curb the power of the big corporations, and laws protecting labor's right to organize, strike, and bargain collectively. But Debs now felt that reform was inadequate.

"The issue is Socialism versus capitalism," he declared in 1897. "I am for Socialism because I am for humanity!"

Until his conversion, the Socialist movement in America had been insignificant, fractured among small groups who constantly argued among themselves. Now many factions followed Debs into a new Socialist Labor Party, which became the Socialist Party of America. Debs sought to persuade Americans to vote capitalism out of existence, replacing it with a Marxian system of public ownership and operation of the means of production and distribution. He scoffed at the timidity of progressives in the major parties who urged slow reforms of capitalism by shorter working hours, unemployment insurance, and government ownership of public utilities.

The Socialists ran Debs for President in 1900—the first of five times. He received a mere 88,000 votes in his first campaign, but by 1912 almost 900,000 Americans were convinced that he was right. In those twelve years, Debs's star rose steadily as journalists known as "muckrakers" began exposing the scandals of big-business corruption. Even two Presidents—Theodore Roosevelt and Woodrow Wilson—felt compelled to denounce the trusts as heartless and vicious.

As early as 1904, however, only Eugene Debs was pointing out the special injustice in American society that was to explode in riots all over the nation over half a century later. "The history of the Negro in the United States," he warned, "is a history of crime without parallel."

Writing in the weekly *Appeal to Reason*, Debs offered Americans a new concept of life, liberty, and the pursuit of happiness. "Every man," he insisted, "has the inalienable right to work." He appealed to workers to close ranks: "You have got to unite in the same labor union and in the same political party and *strike and vote together.* The hour you do that, the world is yours!" He warned them to trust only their solidarity and Socialist understanding, not any leaders.

"I am not a labor leader," he told them. "I don't want you to follow me or anyone else. If you are looking for a Moses to lead you out of the capitalist wilderness, you will stay right where you are. I would not lead you into this promised land if I could, because if I could lead you in, someone else could lead you out!"

He particularly opposed the labor leadership of Samuel Gompers, who believed that the interests of labor and capital were identical, and who was building the American Federation of Labor on a principle of mild craft unionism.

Debs supported, in contrast, the militant Western Federation of Miners, led by tough, one-eyed Big Bill Haywood. To recruit workers for Socialism, he and Haywood organized the Industrial Workers of the World—whose members were soon known as "Wobblies"—in June 1905. But Debs withdrew his support from the IWW when Haywood, instead of using it to educate workers, led the Wobblies in dynamite warfare against Western mine-owners.

By the 1912, elections, over 900,000 Americans wanted Debs's brand of Socialism, but the Democrats rolled up almost seven times as many votes to elect ex-college president Woodrow Wilson. Debs's persistent agitation for social justice had forced the Democrats to steal his thunder by running a liberal reformer who promised Americans a "new freedom."

When war broke out in Europe in 1914, Debs agreed with Wilson's disapproval of "this world war with which we have nothing to do." Debs declared, "No worker has any business to enlist in capitalist class war or fight a capitalist class battle. It is our duty to enlist in our own war and fight our own battle. . . . I have no country to fight for; my country is the earth, and I am a citizen of the world!"

Debs was cynical about the purposes of the war. He saw it as a struggle for commercial markets between English and German capitalists. He knew that munitions merchants like Krupp and Zaharoff were making huge fortunes by arming both sides through neutral nations. Turks slew the British in the Dardanelles with English artillery. The Allies killed Germans with shells made by Krupp workers.

Debs was disgusted when Wilson reluctantly took America into the war in April 1917, following German U-boat warfare against Americans at sea. He was unmoved by government propaganda about "saving the world for democracy" and fighting a "war to end all wars." But his popularity fell sharply as superpatriots and vigilantes began working up mob feeling against those who still dared oppose the war.

Their attacks against Debs reached a peak after the Bolshevik Revolution in Russia because Americans confused Bolshevism with Socialism. "Socialism," accused the Detroit *Journal*, "is Bolshevism with a shave!" When Debs spoke in Canton, Ohio, on June 16, 1918, he knew that Secret Service agents were among the delegates to the Socialist Party Convention.

"I am not opposed," he declared defiantly, "to all wars under all circumstances. . . . I am opposed to every war but one; I am for that war with heart and soul, and that is the world-wide war of social revolution. In that war I am prepared to fight in any way the ruling class may make it necessary, even on the barricades!"

It was then that he was arrested, tried, sentenced to ten years in jail, and deprived of his citizenship. "The government has made me a citizen of the world," he said dryly. When the Supreme Court turned down his appeal, he declared, "The court of final resort is the people, and that court will be heard from in due time."

In 1920 one of the Presidential candidates was Convict 9653, running from his cell in the Atlanta penitentiary. "We nominate him because he has always been the embodiment of all the militant working-class spirit," Morris Hillquit told six thousand cheering Socialist delegates in New York's Madison Square Garden. Debs attacked Harding and Cox as "wings of the same old bird of prey" and urged voters to think deeply about the issues. "I would rather have a man think and vote against me," he asserted, "than give me his vote like a sheep!"

Debs received the greatest acclaim he had ever won—almost 920,000 votes—even while remaining locked in his cell. Petitions for his pardon flooded into the White House.

A 1921 cartoon depicting President Wilson's attitude toward Debs.

"I will never consent to the pardon of this man," Wilson told his aide Joseph Tumulty bitterly. "I know that in certain quarters of this country there is a popular demand for the pardon of Debs. . . . I should never be able to look into the faces of the mothers of this country who sent their boys to the other side. While the flower of American youth was pouring out its blood to vindicate the cause of civilization, this man, Debs, stood behind the lines, sniping, attacking, and denouncing them. . . . Once the Congress of the United States declared war, silence on his part would have been the proper course to pursue. . . . They will say I am cold-blooded and indifferent, but it will make no impression on me. This man was a traitor to his country!"

But on September 5, 1919, Wilson himself admitted to a crowd in St. Louis, "Who does not know that the seed of war in the modern world is industrial and commercial rivalry? The real reason that the war . . . took place was that Germany was afraid her commercial rivals were going to get the better of her, and . . .

they thought Germany would get the commercial advantage of them." Yet he had imprisoned Debs for daring to say the same thing, exposing the war as an imperial struggle for markets, not a crusade for democracy or freedom!

Norman Thomas, who later succeeded Debs as leader of the Socialists, said wryly, "His point-blank refusal to pardon Gene Debs would, if Mr. Wilson were a well man, put the final seal of vindictive animosity upon the career of a man who at the last proved recreant to every high principle of liberalism which he once professed." Ironically, it was the candidate of big business, President Warren Harding, who pardoned Debs in 1921, although not restoring his citizenship.

Debs continued to charge that the ruling classes, who had everything to gain, always brought wars, while workers, who had everything to lose, always fought the battles. He persisted in urging a peaceful transition to Socialism for a better world, and never lost faith in his dream.

"Do you know that all the progress in the whole world's history has been made by minorities?" he declared in 1924. "I have somehow been fortunately all of my life in the minority. I have thought again and again that if I ever find myself in the majority I will know that I have outlived myself. There is something magnificent about having the courage to stand with a few and for a principle and to fight for it . . . no matter whose respect you may forfeit as long as you keep your own!"

He died in Elmhurst, Illinois, on October 20, 1926, one of the most revered of American labor leaders. Many of the abuses of American capitalism of his day have long since been corrected, and rights he demanded for labor have been won. Among the laws he influenced were the Clayton Anti-Trust Act (1914), the Adamson Act (1916), setting an eight-hour day for workers of interstate railroads, and posthumously, the Wagner National Labor Relations Act (1935), requiring employers to recognize and bargain with unions chosen by their workers.

Enough Americans have lost their fear of Socialism to elect many Socialist mayors, councillors, state legislators, and judges. Furthermore, thanks to Debs's courageous struggle, labor leaders today no longer need to cry out as he once did: "Ten thousand times has the labor movement been seized by the throat and choked into insensibility, enjoined by courts, assaulted by thugs, charged by the militia, shot down by regulars, traduced by the press, frowned upon by public opinion, deceived by politicians."

Right or wrong, his courage in going to jail to protest against a war he considered unjust has since made the American government cautious about prosecuting war dissenters. Significantly, no Americans who denounced the Vietnam War as unjust and imperialistic, even as United States troops fought it, were jailed simply for speaking out against it.

Eugene Debs would have considered that progress.

II

"I Believe That Men Will See the Truth"

Woodrow Wilson

He arrived in Paris in December 1918, little over a month after war ended. Two million Frenchmen broke police lines trying to touch his carriage as, with his wife Edith beside him, he was driven down a Champs-Elysées emblazoned in gold letters: HAIL TO WILSON THE JUST!

"Vive Weel-son! Vive Weel-son!"

The French President shouted in his ear, "I do not think there has been anything like it in the history of the world. You are very much loved, *M. le Président!*"

Woodrow Wilson was thrilled, but apprehensive. He had inspired people all over the world by his eloquent appeals for international justice, for a better world tomorrow for all. Now they were convinced that at the peace conference of Versailles, the American President would be able to right all of the world's ancient wrongs. He wrote in a letter home, "What I seem to see—with all my heart I hope that I am wrong—is a tragedy of disappointment!"

Determined above all to create a League of Nations that would prevent any more world wars, he was warned that Prime Minister Lloyd George of England would never agree to it.

"Then I shall look him in the eye," Wilson vowed, "and say to him, 'Damn you, if you will not accept the League of Nations,

I shall go to the people of Great Britain and say things to them which will shake your Government!'"

It was not Lloyd George who destroyed his hopes for the League, however, but Wilson's fellow Americans.

Thomas Woodrow Wilson, who later dropped his first name, was born December 28, 1856, in Staunton, Virginia. His mother was a minister's daughter, his father a Presbyterian minister. Young Wilson was deeply influenced by his father's scholarship, faith, eloquence, and wit. At Princeton he prepared himself for a career in government economy and politics. Personal shyness made him seem cold, aloof, and arrogant to classmates, but he had a warm relationship with a few close friends.

In his senior year his studies convinced him of a fundamental weakness in American democracy—the ability of a few powerful committee chairmen in Congress to block reform bills by burying them in committee. He made "Cabinet Government" his senior thesis, and later developed it into a book *The Nation* called "one of the most important books dealing with political subjects ever issued from the American press."

He finished his training at the University of Virginia Law School and Johns Hopkins University. After a brief and unsuccessful fling at the law, he taught history and political science at Bryn Mawr, Wesleyan, and finally at his alma mater, Princeton. Here his achievements as an educator and speaker were so brilliant that in 1902, at the age of forty-six, he became the university's first non-clerical president. By this time he had a devoted wife, Ellen, and three daughters.

He soon stunned the Board of Trustees by insisting on revolutionizing Princeton's educational system, changing it from a snobbish haven for rich men's sons into a democratic community of enthusiastic scholars. When the Board tried to stop him, he made the fight public and broadened it to a general attack on the unfairness of privilege in American society.

Woodrow Wilson hails a cheering Paris as he rides through the streets alongside the French President.

"The American people will tolerate nothing that savors of exclusiveness," he insisted. He told a dinner of the nation's top financiers, "You bankers are too narrow-minded. . . . There is a higher law than the law of profits!" He lashed out at religious leaders for toadying to the wealthy: "The Protestant churches are serving the classes and not the masses!" His reputation grew steadily as an impressive fighter against the forces of the rich and snobbish.

Seeing Wilson as a popular vote-getter, the Democrats of New Jersey ran him for Governor in 1910, and he was elected. Party bosses were shocked when he refused them special favors and insisted upon carrying out campaign pledges to end the state's notorious corruption. His reform administration made New Jersey a widely praised model state.

In 1912, the national Democratic Party made him their Presidential candidate against Republican Taft and Progressive Theodore Roosevelt. Wilson charged the Republicans with being tools of the big corporations, and Roosevelt as being too radical. Offering himself as a liberal reformer who would bring Americans a "New Freedom," he won.

Intending to be a strong President, he chose a weak cabinet that would do his bidding. "What's the point of suggesting ideas to Wilson," one cabinet aide grumbled, "when he already *knows* all the answers?" He also lectured Senators like a schoolmaster. One Senator protested, "Mr. President, don't you allow others to disagree with you?" He replied, "I feel sorry for them, because I know they are wrong!"

He forced Congress to stay in session during a blistering Washington summer until they passed the "New Freedom" reforms he demanded. New laws forced down prices to consumers by lowering tariffs on foreign imports; broke the Wall Street money monopoly; protected little shopowners from unfair chain store competition; broke up powerful trusts; improved conditions at sea for merchant seamen; reduced child labor; gave railroad workers an eight-hour day; gave farmers cheap, long-term credit.

Wilson's domestic program was everything he had promised to the American people. But he blundered badly when he tried to introduce idealism into United States foreign policy.

Determined to end United States interference in Latin American affairs, he warned Wall Street that United States bayonets would no longer be allowed to back up foreign investments. Such dollar imperialism, he charged, was "obnoxious to the principles upon which the government of our people rests." Offering Colombia an official apology and a twenty-million-dollar indemnity for Theodore Roosevelt's seizure of their land to build the Panama Canal, he vowed, "The United States will never again seek one additional foot of territory by conquest!"

But he was outraged when the new Mexican President, Francisco Madero, was ousted and murdered by bandit general Victoriano Huerta. To overthrow the Huerta dictatorship and restore popular government in Mexico, Wilson supported a rival general, Carranza, and his bandit chieftain ally, Pancho Villa. United States Marines were ordered to occupy Veracruz. Finally, in July 1914, Huerta was forced to flee to Spain.

To Wilson's dismay, Carranza and Villa then began to fight each other for power. Both also attacked Americans and United States property in Mexico, reflecting Mexican indignation over the Marines still in Veracruz. Perplexed, Wilson ended the occupation and recognized a new Carranza government. Villa retaliated by a raid across the New Mexico border that killed twenty Americans. Wilson angrily sent an expeditionary force into Mexico under Pershing to capture Villa.

Carranza, in turn, grew indignant at this new violation of Mexican sovereignty, and his troops compelled Pershing's forces to retreat. United States Senators stormed into the White House to demand war against Mexico. Wilson stunned them by asking them to pledge that *their* sons would enlist.

"Do you think the glory of America would be enhanced by a war with Mexico?" he challenged them. "Do you think that any act of violence by a powerful nation like this against a weak and distracted neighbor would reflect distinction upon the United States?" He was distressed when liberal critics attacked from the opposite direction, calling his intervention in Mexico as reprehensible as previous United States military adventures south of the border.

"Mistakes I have no doubt made in this perplexing business," he admitted, "but not in purpose or object!"

In August 1914, as his wife Ellen lay dying, the distraught Wilson was forced to formulate American policy toward the outbreak of world war in Europe. Suppressing personal sympathies for the British, he called upon the American people to be "neutral in fact as well as in name."

In 1915 he declared, "We shall not turn America into a military camp. We will not ask our young men to spend the best years of their lives making soldiers of themselves!" But as Germany answered his loans and supply shipments to the Allies by unrestricted U-boat warfare at sea, he reluctantly authorized a "preparedness" program. He confided his anxiety about being dragged into the war to Edith Boiling Galt, a Washington widow who became his second wife.

The Democratic slogan, "He kept us out of the war," won reelection for Wilson in 1916. He refused to make that pledge personally. "Why, at any moment," he told an aide, "some little German lieutenant may do something that will force me to lead the nation to war!" Then Germany, compelled by Wilson to promise to respect the lives of Americans at sea, broke that promise. On April 6, 1917, a pale Wilson asked Congress for a declaration of war against Germany—not in revenge, but because "the world must be made safe for democracy!"

A storm of applause swept Congress and the gallery.

Returning to his office, Woodrow Wilson wept.

"Think what it was they were applauding," he whispered to his aide Joseph Tumulty. "My message today was a message of death for our young men. How strange it seems to applaud that!" So the President who had vowed to keep Americans at peace led them into the hell of the First World War, a war he *had* to believe was a just war for noble goals.

But when the Bolsheviks seized power in Russia, captured files of the Czar revealed secret Allied treaties, exposing the war as a sordid struggle for spoils among capitalist powers. Lenin took Russia out of the war and published the secret treaties. "Why fight an imperialist war which has nothing to do with you except as cannon fodder?" he asked workers on both sides through *Izvestia*. "The American President Wilson, adopting the tone of a Quaker preacher, came into the war because of the interests of the New York Stock Exchange!" Upset, Wilson pressured England and France to refute Lenin in the court of world opinion by joining him in an idealistic statement of Allied war aims. They refused.

So Wilson drew up a program of Fourteen Points for a just peace, and on his own proclaimed these to the world as the war goals of the Allies. The Fourteen Points lifted hearts and hopes in every part of the globe. They weakened the German people's will to fight, convincing them that Wilson was not against them but only their tyrannical overlords. The Germans finally surrendered, ending a terrible war that had killed or wounded almost thirty million soldiers.

Determined to write the Fourteen Points into the peace treaty, Wilson asked the American people to show the world they supported him by electing a Democratic majority in Congress in the off-year elections of 1918. Instead, a war-weary public gave the Republicans control of both Houses. Wilson's arch foe, Henry Cabot Lodge, became head of the Senate Foreign Relations Committee and a power on Capitol Hill.

Stunned, Wilson nevertheless determined to lead the American peace delegation to Versailles himself. "There are many questions coming up between the Allies which threaten friction," he declared defiantly, "and I am the only man in the world who can straighten them out!"

Yet even as he sailed for Europe, Theodore Roosevelt roared in the press, "Our allies and our enemies and Mr. Wilson himself should all understand that Mr. Wilson has no authority whatever to speak for the American people at this time. His leadership has just been emphatically repudiated by them." It was an open invitation to Lloyd George and Clemenceau to reject the Fourteen Points, including the League of Nations Wilson wanted as a guardian of world peace.

He was given wildly enthusiastic receptions all over Europe—Paris, London, Italy. "I am afraid they are going to be disappointed," he told physician-aide Cary Grayson, "and turn about and hiss me." It was an accurate prophecy.

At Versailles Wilson clashed constantly with Clemenceau, who groaned, *Mon Dieu!* Wilson with his Fourteen Points is

Lloyd George, Count Orlando, Clemenceau, and Wilson at Versailles.

worse than God Almighty—who had only ten!" The American President refused to let his Allies grab Germany's colonies as spoils or plant the seeds of a war of revenge by impoverishing Germans under staggering war debts. He finally won their agreement to most of his Fourteen Points.

But news from home revealed a high tide of Republican opposition to United States membership in the League. Wilson hurried home to answer Senate objections to Article X of the treaty, the League Covenant. Lodge let him think it would be approved with amendments guaranteeing the United States the right to quit and jurisdiction over disputes under the Monroe Doctrine.

Returning to Europe, Wilson told Edith gloomily, "It's impossible to satisfy everyone. Oppressed minorities everywhere expect me to protect them. Our own people expect me to make a League of Nations work without obligating them to anything. Clemenceau and Lloyd George want me to respect their secret treaties. Germany expects me to guarantee them a just peace. Only God knows how to satisfy them all—I certainly don't!" So he prayed to his God for guidance.

Back at the Peace Conference, he worked day and night, ruining his health in a desperate effort to win the new concessions demanded by the Senate without paying a heavy price in war spoils to his Allies. Compromising as little as possible, he finally forced agreement on a treaty by threatening to walk out on the Peace Conference.

His departure, as he had predicted, was marked by only token crowds and a few scattered cheers. Disappointed French, British, and Italians felt he had deprived them of war reparations. He reached home to find bored Americans sick of the postwar problems of Europe, convinced by Lodge that he had submerged United States sovereignty under a world power. The President's "high-falutin', holier-than-thou" personality now seemed to irritate his fellow Americans, who were weary of idealistic preaching and sacrifices, yearning only for the carefree "return to normalcy" the Republicans were promising.

Lodge now decided to kill the League Covenant in the treaty by amending it to death. He knew that Wilson would not and could not accept such amendments, and he was right. They fought a fierce press duel through the hot summer months of 1919. Finally Wilson, in despair, decided to tour the country personally and arouse his fellow Americans to the danger of a Second World War if Lodge and the Senate were not forced to ratify the League and the treaty.

Dr. Grayson begged the ailing President not to make the tour; it could kill him. "I *must* go, Grayson!" Wilson replied. "The League is in crisis. If it fails, I hate to think what will happen to the world. The soldiers I sent into the trenches didn't turn back. Neither can I. . . . I don't care if I die one minute after the treaty is ratified. I will gladly forfeit my life to attain the end I seek!"

On September 3, 1919, he set out on a strenuous speech-making train tour of forty key cities. Following him around the country, Republican Senators denounced the League as "that evil thing with the holy name." The country found itself caught up in the greatest controversy since the Lincoln-Douglas debates. The Republicans accused the President of ambitions to become the uncrowned king of the world.

"Who betrayed the American soldier and American ideals?" roared Senator William Borah in Chicago. The crowd thundered, "Wilson! Impeach Wilson!" The President lashed back by telling Americans, "If you do not want little groups of selfish men to plot the future of Europe, we must not allow little groups of selfish men to plot the future of America!"

On September 25, speaking at Pueblo, Colorado, to a crowd of ten thousand, he said, "I believe that men will see the truth . . . and it is going to lead us, and through us the world, out into pastures of quietness and peace such as the world never dreamed of before." There was a hush, broken by muffled sobs, such as the reverent awe Moses might have inspired urging his followers on to the Promised Land.

But that night Woodrow Wilson collapsed with a stroke that partially paralyzed his left side. The Presidential train headed mournfully back to Washington, bearing its fallen warrior. For almost two months his condition was kept secret from the country, with Edith Wilson serving as his surrogate. But even now his wry wit did not fail him.

Lodge dispatched Senator Albert Fall to the White House on an "urgent" pretext, to spy on and report Wilson's "incompetence." Fall declared piously, "Mr. President, I want you to know that I am praying for you."

"Which way, Senator," Wilson murmured, "which way?"

He refused to compromise with any of Lodge's fourteen reservations to the League, which he knew would nullify it. When Lodge forced the reservations into the treaty submitted to the

A 1919 cartoon from the *Tribune* entitled, "Discussing the League To Enforce Peace."

full Senate, Wilson ordered Democrats to vote the treaty down. So the League of Nations came into being without the support or participation of the American government that had proposed it. This weakness eventually killed it, leading to the Second World War Wilson had warned against.

The American people, who had followed Lodge instead of Wilson, were given a second chance in the elections of 1920. James M. Cox, running as the Democratic Presidential candidate against Republican Warren Harding, waged his campaign as a "great and solemn referendum" to let the people express their feelings about the League directly. They voted overwhelmingly for Harding—sixteen million to Cox's nine million—a stunning humiliation and repudiation for Wilson.

"The people will have to learn now by bitter experience," he commented sadly, "just what they have lost. . . . Soon we will be witnessing the tragedy of it all!" Retiring to private life, he was awarded the Nobel Peace Prize in 1920. But he died broken and rejected, a prophet spurned by his people, on February 3, 1924. He had a final prophecy in his last public appearance three months before his death:

"I am not one of those who have the least anxiety about the triumph of the principles I have stood for. I have seen fools resist Providence before, and I have seen their destruction, as will come upon these again. . . . That *we* shall prevail is as sure as that God reigns!"

When the terrible Second World War he had predicted broke out in 1939, Americans knew they had been wrong in spurning the wisdom of Woodrow Wilson. They were given the final chance that he had predicted in San Francisco on June 26, 1945. This time the United States joined with forty-six other nations of the world in a new and stronger league of nations designed to prevent another world war—the United Nations.

Thomas Connally, ranking chief delegate next to the Secretary of State at that historic conference, declared, "It was generally and definitely recognized that the organization created there was a reflection of the high purposes of Woodrow Wilson. . . . His inspiration prompted its adoption by the United States Senate and the American people."

Woodrow Wilson had not given his life in vain.

12

First Female Doctor in the West

Bethenia Owens

In the Oregon of the 1870s, Dr. Bethenia Owens outraged every male concept of what a woman ought to be. This scandalous female was not only a divorcee, but even dared hang out her shingle as the only woman doctor in the entire West.

Obviously she needed a lesson, and her fellow doctors of Roseburg, Oregon, intended to see that she got it. In small Western towns of those days, public autopsies served to provide morbid entertainment for bored males. One autopsy on an old derelict who had died of unknown causes was scheduled a few days after Bethenia opened her practice in Roseburg. Fifty men and boys crowded into the autopsy shed to watch the town's six male doctors perform the operation.

"Wait a minute, gentlemen," said a sardonic doctor named Palmer. "We must not be discourteous to our lady colleague in town. I suggest she be invited to be present!"

Whoops of approving laughter shook the shed. Dr. Palmer scribbled a note and gave it to a boy to deliver to Bethenia at her office. The amused male doctors knew that she would not dare to show up. What woman would humiliate herself by being present at the dissection of an undraped male body, with fifty men observing her reactions?

Roseburg's new lady doctor read the note with cool detachment. She was well aware of the intended mockery, reflecting the intense resentment male physicians felt for a female who dared invade a traditionally all-male profession.

"Give the doctors my compliments," she told the boy who had brought the note. "Say I'll be there in a minute."

The news created disbelief at first, then a gale of mirthful anticipation. The shed grew hushed as Bethenia appeared, a quiet-looking, pleasant woman in her thirties. Her hair was worn out of the way in a wad under a doll-sized bonnet, and her overskirt was simple and businesslike.

A doctor named Hoover hurried toward her, blocking out her view of the body on the table. "Do you realize," he warned her, "that the autopsy will involve *all* parts of the body?"

"One part of the human body, Doctor," she said calmly, "should be as sacred to the physician as another."

At this Dr. Palmer could not contain his indignation.

"I *object* to a woman's being present at a male autopsy. If she is allowed to remain, then I shall retire!"

Bethenia Owens's eyes flashed. "I came here by your own written invitation, Doctor. Since you now object, may I ask you to explain the difference between the attendance of a woman physician at a male autopsy, and the attendance of a man physician at a female autopsy?" His jaw dropped.

She turned to the other doctors. "However, I am willing to leave it to a vote of your colleagues. Gentlemen?"

The other five physicians, both abashed and impressed, voted to allow her to remain. Dr. Palmer stalked out of the shed in a rage. One of the doctors opened his case of surgical instruments and held it out to Bethenia. Without the slightest hesitation she took the case, approached the table, and calmly performed the autopsy with expert precision.

The fifty men in the shed watched in spellbound silence. There was not a smothered laugh or jeer. Afterward, as the doctors nodded to indicate that she had done the job well, the shed exploded with wild excitement and cheers.

On her way home, however, she found the streets of Roseburg lined with hostile men, women, and children. The story had spread through town. Everyone wanted to stare at the brazen woman who had dared to do what she had. Men wore contemptuous smirks. Women were scandalized. There was angry talk of tar and feathers, of running the outrageous young lady doctor out of town, of putting her in jail.

"I believe all that saved me was the fact that my brothers lived there," she recalled later. "And as everybody knew they would shoot at the drop of a hat, good care was taken to lay no violent hands on me." But public feeling against Bethenia Owens ran so high that she could get no patients and was compelled to leave Roseburg.

Her parents were pioneers who came west to Oregon over the rugged Rocky Mountain Trail in 1843, when she was three. At the age of fourteen she married an idler named Legrand Hill, who preferred hunting to completing a log hut for his wife and son. She had to share her kitchen with skunks who came in every night under the open flooring, rattling the pots and eating everything in sight.

Bethenia and her baby, George, both suffered from typhoid. Even more of an ordeal was her husband's vicious temper. When the baby's fever caused him to cry, Hill would beat him unmercifully. Anguished, Bethenia warned her husband she would leave him unless he stopped beating their child. One night the baby was too sick to eat. Exasperated, Hill forced him to swallow six hard-boiled eggs. When Bethenia tried to stop him, he struck and choked her. The baby regurgitated. Furious, Hill threw him on the bed, punched him, then raged off into town. Bethenia could stand no more.

Swiftly bundling up little George, she fled back to her parents' home. The future looked bleak. Only eighteen now,

THE COMING RACE.

Doctor Evangeline. "BY THE BYE, MR. SAWYER, ARE YOU ENGAGED TO-MORROW AFTERNOON? I HAVE RATHER A TICKLISH OPERATION TO PERFORM—AN AMPUTATION, YOU KNOW."

Mr. Sawyer. "I SHALL BE VERY HAPPY TO DO IT FOR YOU."

Dr. Evangeline. "O, NO, NOT *THAT*! BUT WILL YOU KINDLY COME AND ADMINISTER THE CHLOROFORM FOR ME?"

Men were reluctant to accept women physicians as their equals in medical skill.

Bethenia somehow had to provide for her sickly child in a world that regarded divorcees as hardly more respectable than "fallen women." With the additional handicaps of ill health and lack of education, Bethenia decided that her only hope lay in returning to school. Her mother agreed to look after the baby while she returned to the classroom with her younger brothers and sisters.

She studied so determinedly that she completed three years' work in four months, even while doing the whole family's washing and ironing. All through her twenties she kept going to school, supporting herself and little George by milking cows, washing, ironing, picking berries, sewing, teaching summer school, and working as a practical nurse.

She would rise at dawn, work until schooltime, go to school with George, work again until dark, then study until 2 a.m. by the guttering light of homemade candles, ironing as she studied. She and George boarded from place to place, living wherever it was cheapest. They kept warm by fires of driftwood they collected together on the beach.

Bethenia was often exhausted, but her desire for education was so overwhelming that death alone could have swerved her. Deeply impressed, a kindly old Columbia River captain offered to underwrite the rest of her education, and George's, too, with no strings attached. Tears of gratitude sprang to her eyes. But much to his vexation, she refused. Her pride in self-reliance was too strong to permit Bethenia Owens to feel beholden to anyone.

Her interest in medicine began as a result of hiring out as a practical nurse. In those days that meant not only looking after a sick woman, but also serving her family—and hired farmhands—as cook, laundress, milkmaid, and cleaning woman. Once, after three weeks of working for a farmer named Kelly, he balked at paying the five dollars a week she asked.

"Three is plenty for woman's work!" he snapped. Bethenia was indignant at this display of contempt for her sex. The incident long rankled in her memory, influencing her later fight for equal rights for women. She vowed, "The time will come when that man Kelly will be glad to acknowledge my superiority!" And come it did.

Some years later, when she was on a train bound for the state capital, surrounded by many prominent figures, a man broke through the group, eager to talk to the famous Dr. Bethenia Owens. It was Kelly. When he reminded her who he was, she nodded politely, then returned to conversing with her distinguished companions. The embarrassed farmer, who had once considered three dollars a week "plenty" for women's work, slunk off red-faced.

Bethenia's decision to become a doctor took place in 1870. She had made some money by opening a millinery shop, and had sent George off to the University of California. But she had continued to do nursing on the side because she enjoyed it. One night a friend with a very sick child sent for her.

Dr. Palmer was in attendance. He was unsuccessful in using an instrument to relieve the child's suffering, causing it to scream in pain by his clumsiness. Irked, he put down the instrument to wipe his glasses. "Let me try, Doctor," Bethenia urged. Before he could protest, she had done the job easily, smoothly, and successfully. The mother threw her arms around Bethenia's neck and wept her appreciation.

Dr. Palmer froze. "Impudence!" he snarled. "Before you ever dare do anything like that again, bring along your medical degree!"

That, Bethenia vowed angrily, was exactly what she *would* do. Selling her millinery shop, she announced that she was going to a medical college. Her family felt disgraced. Not long before, a mob had thrown rotten eggs at some female medical students in Philadelphia. A newspaper had applauded their action, declaring sanctimoniously, "No modest or refined woman would study medicine!" Women who had bought hats from Bethenia said frostily, "Please do not expect us to consult a *woman* as a physician!"

Bethenia announced firmly, "The delicate and sympathetic office of a physician belongs more to our sex than the other. I intend to enter it and make it an honor to women."

She won her MD at the University of Michigan. Soon after the autopsy incident in Roseburg, when Dr. Palmer sought to humiliate her, she spent all her savings traveling around Europe for three years. Visiting the best hospitals in every country, she watched the world's greatest surgeons operate. She never tired of learning.

Returning to Oregon with only two hundred dollars left, she so impressed a Portland doctor with her knowledge that he sold her his practice and equipment on credit. Despite the widespread prejudice against, and the unpopularity of, lady doctors, Bethenia's medical skill was soon the talk of Portland. Women flocked to her office in ever-increasing numbers.

She was always ready to drop everything and fly to the bedside of any woman who needed her urgently. Once a frantic husband rushed into her inner office, yelling that his wife was dying. She flew off in her buggy, the husband at her side as she lashed out at the horses. Suddenly they were brought up short by the frantic signaling of two of Bethenia's sisters. Reining in the horses to the curb, she panted, "What's the matter?"

"Bethenia! You have no *hat!*"

She lashed out at the horses again. As they flew on she said crossly to the husband, "Why didn't you tell me I was bareheaded? Do you want to ruin my reputation?" But he couldn't reply because he was holding on for dear life, petrified by her headlong dash. The patient, as she had rather suspected, proved not to be seriously ill. After attending to her, Bethenia borrowed one of her old hats and drove back to the office "respectably" attired.

Her tremendous energy spilled over from medicine into the field of social welfare. One day in 1882, an embarrassed young man asked her if she would attend a sick girl in a frankly disreputable section of town. She didn't hesitate.

"I never refuse to visit any suffering person who needs help," she replied. "I'll go and do all I can."

She was shocked to find that the girl was only fifteen, and seriously ill with peritonitis. Bethenia had her moved to a comfortable room near her, and kept her under personal care and treatment. She then found a kind woman to take the girl into her home and keep her there until she was well enough to return home to her mother.

Disturbed by the tragic plight of girls rejected by society for their mistakes, Bethenia crusaded for funds to build a Refuge Home for unwed mothers. Today this is the Florence Crittenton Home. To prevent the further misery of other young girls, Bethenia addressed the Oregon legislature in 1889. At her insistence it passed a bill raising the age of consent to sixteen years, making men wary of taking advantage of the ignorance of young girls under that age.

Ever the courageous rebel, Bethenia was never afraid to challenge public statements made by some of America's most respected authorities. President Eliot of Harvard assured worried parents that their college sons' postgraduate studies were "conducive to celibacy." Laughed Bethenia, "He's crazy!" Eliot claimed athletics would injure a girl for life.

"Twaddle!" she scoffed. "It adds to her strength, her beauty, her usefulness, and her longevity." When Portland officials proposed banning the city's ice-skating rink to girls as "too rough" for them, Bethenia pointed out acidly that most girls were too coddled already: "If any of these young ladies were required to walk briskly a mile and a half, she would be sure to have an attack of neuralgia or a 'nervous chill'!"

She did not hesitate to speak out loudly and clearly against those austere church authorities who stigmatized babies born out of wedlock as "children of sin."

"I never heard of such hypocritical cruelty to innocent babies!" she flared. "How *dare* they call themselves Christians!"

At forty-four, Bethenia met and married Colonel John Adair, by whom she had a daughter. But the infant lived only three days. Saddened and in ill health, Bethenia retreated to her husband's farm for eleven years. Throughout this time she answered the calls of the sick in the blackest of nights and fiercest of storms. Often the dense trails and flooded tidelands were so muddy that no horse could get through. Bethenia, her boots filled with water, drenched to the skin, would stumble and fall for miles by lantern-light to reach a sick person who needed her.

Once a storm was so wild that trees were falling like matchsticks under its fury. Colonel Adair refused to let his wife risk her life to ride through it to a patient.

"I promised to go," she insisted, "and I *must* go."

He finally gave in, but fastened harnesses from her shoulders to the saddle so that the storm could not blow her off her horse. Then away she galloped on her errand of mercy.

There was no end to her courage. Once when there was Indian trouble in the county, twenty warriors suddenly appeared at the Adair farmhouse. While her husband went out to talk to them, Bethenia stood in the doorway with a shotgun in her hands, ready to use it if Adair were attacked.

On another occasion she came across a burly man beating an old woman senseless. Outraged, she demanded, "Let that woman alone, you brute!" He sprang for her drunkenly with outstretched hands. She snatched a whip from a wagon, and hit him with the iron-loaded butt. He knocked her down and would have killed her if help had not arrived.

In 1905, when she was sixty-five, she exhausted herself fighting a diphtheria epidemic in the state of Washington. "During sixty consecutive hours," reported a Washington newspaper, "Dr. Owens accomplished an almost incredible amount of labor—

having traveled in that time over 100 miles, with but two hours' sleep out of the whole sixty hours—a record very few male physicians, if any, could equal and surely none could excel."

When the American Medical Association paid its first recognition to women physicians by giving them a banquet in Portland, one of Bethenia's colleagues told her, "Why, Doctor, you look like a bride in that white dress!"

"I feel like one," she laughed. "For this day, in which I finally see all our efforts bearing fruit, is the happiest in my life. I thank God that I have been spared to see the day when women are acknowledged before the world as the equal of men in medicine and surgery!"

For over a century, millions of Americans have benefited from the healing talents of the nation's women physicians. Few women made it more possible than the courageous pioneer whose daring made her so unpopular that she was driven out of town.

13

"The Law Was Wrong, Not I"

Margaret Sanger

On January 29, 1917, as an anxious nation waited to see whether President Wilson would declare war, a slight little woman faced three frowning judges in a Brooklyn, New York, courtroom. Fifty immigrant women clutched fruit, bread, and babies as they waited anxiously for a chance to help their angel of mercy, Mrs. Margaret Sanger. One by one they testified eagerly how the defendant had helped the sick, the desperately poor, the mothers who had had ten live and three dead children.

They thought they were saving her. Instead, they were dooming her to jail for violating Section 1142 of the New York Penal Code, which prohibited dissemination of birth control information, and Section 1530, which forbade "maintaining a public nuisance"—in her case the first Planned Parenthood clinic in the United States.

"Margaret Sanger, stand up!"

She faced the bench, her heart pounding. Would she, the Court demanded, solemnly promise not to violate the law again? No, she replied defiantly, she would not.

"I can't respect the law as it stands today," she said.

The judges bristled. "You have challenged the constitutionality of the law under consideration and the jurisdiction of this Court. . . . Refusal to obey the law becomes open defiance

Margaret Sanger worked among people who begged her to reveal the secret of curbing childbearing.

of the rule of the majority. . . . The judgment of the Court is that you be confined to the Workhouse for a period of thirty days."

"Shame!" cried out a horrified woman spectator. The gavel banged angrily and the prisoner was led away.

"I was combating a mass ideology and the judges who were its spokesmen," she wrote later. Anything but a cooperative prisoner, she refused to be fingerprinted or medically examined. A woman attendant at the Raymond Street jail sneered, "One of the fighting kind, are you? Well, we'll soon fix you, young lady!" She vanished for instructions. Reappearing, her voice was respectful: "Oh, you're Mrs. Sanger! It's all right. Come this way, please."

Transferred to the Queens County penitentiary at Long Island City, she lived for a month with female pickpockets, embezzlers, thieves, prostitutes, and drug addicts. Discovering that many were illiterate, she helped them read and write their letters.

She was deeply moved when a visiting friend showed her a letter from one of the immigrant women she had helped:

"We women here want to find out what the President, the Mayor, and the Judges and everybody is trying to do. First they put Mrs. Sanger in jail for telling us women how not to have any more children, and then they get busy for the starve of the ones we've got. . . . The children are living on bread and tea leaves that is kept cooking on the back of the stove. Honest to God, we ought to call a meeting and do something!"

She was treated well in prison except during the final hours, when the warden ordered her fingerprints taken forcibly. Struggling, she was weak and exhausted when a phone call came ordering her immediate release. She emerged from the jail, arms bruised but triumphant, to be greeted by a group of admiring friends singing the *Marseillaise*.

She was born Margaret Higgins, of Irish parents, in Corning, New York, on September 14, 1883. Her nonconformist father, a Civil War veteran, raised eleven children—Margaret was the sixth—by carving tombstone angels and saints. "Our existence was like that of any artist's family," Margaret recalled. "Chickens today and feathers tomorrow."

Once her father arranged for the atheist Robert G. Ingersoll to speak at the Corning Town Hall, and took Margaret and the older children to hear him. The meeting was broken up by hurled tomatoes, apples, and cabbages—"my first experience of rage," she noted, "directed against those holding views which were contrary to accepted ones." Because of her father's sponsorship of Ingersoll, the Higgins youngsters became known as "children of the Devil," and were forced to endure the jeers and ostracism of other youngsters.

Margaret worked her way through Claverack College and Hudson River Institute by waiting on tables and washing dishes. Returning home to nurse her mother, who was dying of tuberculosis, she borrowed medical books from the local doctor. Studying about tuberculosis, she became interested in medicine. After her mother's death she was accepted as a probationer at White Plains Hospital nursing school.

Night duty brought some harrowing experiences with psychotic patients. One man lunged at her with a knife. Gripping his wrist, she escaped death only because illness had left him weak. He proved to be a gangster wanted for five murders. Another deranged patient asked her for a drink, then knocked her ten feet against a wall, choking her until an orderly finally came dashing to her rescue.

Called out in the middle of the night on maternity cases, she often had to deliver the baby herself when the doctor was late. Many poor mothers begged her for advice in avoiding subsequent pregnancies. She would refer them to the doctor, but he would just shrug. Margaret began to feel that there was something seriously wrong about compelling women to be mothers against their will, especially those with more babies than they could feed and clothe properly, or who were too ill to look after the families they already had.

And was it fair to the babies themselves to let them come into the world unwanted, with little chance of the loving care and opportunities that all children deserved?

Concluding her training at the Manhattan Eye and Ear Hospital in New York, Margaret met and married a Socialist architect, William Sanger. They had three children, who were often looked after by her mother-in-law as Margaret pursued her nursing career. Joining her husband in the Socialist Party, she was asked to give health talks to women's groups. Young mothers kept asking her questions about conjugal relations—questions no one else was answering.

Margaret finally wrote a series of articles on sex information for mothers and daughters in the *Socialist Call.* But one day, under the title *What Every Girl Should Know,* there was only white space with the message: "NOTHING—by order of the Post Office Department." The censored article had explained the dangers of venereal disease. Anthony Comstock, head of the New York Society for the Suppression of Vice, forced the Post Office to forbid the *Call* to run any more "lewd, lascivious, indecent and obscene" articles.

Working as a visiting nurse on the Lower East Side, Margaret attended poor, uneducated women having babies at home.

In every slum tenement flat she visited, neighbors brought her gifts, hoping to bribe her to reveal the "secret" of curbing continuous childbearing. She brooded over the legal ban against teaching them the means of fertility control. Doctors called it a social problem; social workers called it a medical problem. Meanwhile, thousands of wretched women followed old wives' tales in seeking to end unwanted pregnancies by dangerous or useless techniques that killed some and crippled many others for life.

One hot night in July 1912, Margaret was called to attend a poor Russian immigrant with three children who was close to death as a result of trying to end a fourth pregnancy. "Please tell me the secret of not having any more children," she wept on Margaret's shoulder, "and I'll never breathe it to a soul. *Please!*" She died three months later. Her husband tore his hair, wailing, "My God! My God!"

That night Margaret Sanger knew that, whatever the cost to herself, she must do something to end the plight of poor mothers "whose miseries were as vast as the sky."

In order to learn how other countries were handling the problem, she went to Europe in 1913 with her husband and children. By the end of the year she had learned much—but at a high personal cost. Her obsession was too remote from her husband's interests. They decided to divorce, and William Sanger remained behind in Paris to paint.

Returning home, Margaret rounded up some sympathetic friends and organized the National Birth Control League. In 1914, she published the first issue of a magazine called *The Woman Rebel,* its slogan "No Gods, No Masters," its alleged objective "To stimulate working women to think for themselves and to build up a conscious fighting character."

Chief among its "rebel thoughts" was the advocacy of birth control, and the right of the League to give this information freely to women. Powerful pressures were swiftly brought to bear, and *The Woman Rebel* was barred from the mails, leaving Margaret heavily in debt. "To me it was outrageous," she declared indignantly, "that information regarding motherhood, which was so generally called sacred, should be classed with pornography!"

Among the powerful forces that considered Margaret Sanger well intentioned but misguided was the Catholic Church. The Church did not condone any of the shocking conditions that upset her, but believed that birth control was the wrong answer, besides violating Catholic teaching about the sanctity of human conception. The leading Church opponent of Margaret's National Birth Control League was Archbishop Patrick J. Hayes, who expressed his views in a Christmas Pastoral:

"Children troop down from Heaven because God wills it. He alone has the right to stay their coming, while He blesses at will some homes with many, others with but few or none at all. . . . To prevent human life that the Creator is about to bring into being is satanic. . . . an immortal soul is denied existence in time and in eternity. It has been reserved to our day to see advocated shamelessly the legalizing of such a diabolical thing."

Modern Catholic doctrine is perhaps better expressed by Father John L. Thomas, one of America's leading authorities on family relationships: "God alone is the Author and source of life. . . . [Humans] may not place a direct, antecedent obstacle to hinder the natural physiological process of the reproductive act . . . [which] has been entrusted to men and women for the good of the species, and right reason demands that it be employed accordingly."

Opposition to the National Birth Control League also came from the business world, for economic reasons. Margaret Sanger had made it clear that it was the working classes who most desperately needed to reduce the size of their families. Fewer babies meant fewer workers; a labor shortage would compel higher wages and shorter hours.

When *The Woman Rebel* was barred from the mails, Margaret wrote a pamphlet called *Family Limitation*. But twenty New York printers she approached were all afraid of prosecution under the same Comstock Act of 1873 that made it a crime to send "obscene literature" through the mails. Frustrated, she decided to defy the law and talked the printer of *The Woman Rebel* into putting out another issue with the same information. She was promptly placed under arrest.

Her father, who had at first scoffed at her crusade, now came to her support after reading the issue. "Your mother would have been alive today," he admitted somberly, "if we had just known all of this then!" But the Post Office Department was determined that she must be convicted.

Her lawyer urged her to plead guilty, assuring her he could get her off with a light fine. She refused, explaining that she had deliberately violated the law to test it. "I was trying to prove," she wrote later, "the law was wrong, not I." She was deeply anxious about what might happen to her children if she were forced to go to jail, but even that worry could not shake her determination.

"I was not afraid of the penitentiary," she recalled. "I was not afraid of anything except being misunderstood."

She asked for a postponement of her trial to give her time to prepare an adequate defense. The Court denied it. Indignant, she postponed the trial herself by leaving for Montreal without a passport. Sympathizers in Canada not only gave her refuge, but also helped arrange publication of *Family Limitation* for smuggling into the United States.

They sent her on to England to prepare her defense with the aid of studies in the British Museum. She also talked with Havelock Ellis and other English rebels who had fought bouts with British censorship. A visit to Holland gave her the opportunity to study that little country's Planned Parenthood clinics, and she learned that they had sharply reduced both maternal and infant deaths.

Ready to face trial, she returned home in September 1915 with new insights. Educating women was not enough. She must establish clinics of personal instruction, like Holland's, throughout the United States. But she found that in her absence the National Birth Control League had been reorganized under Mary Ware Dennett, who disagreed with her defiance of the law to force a test and who would not support her.

Once more her lawyer urged her to plead guilty and promise to respect the law in the future so he could keep her from going to jail. "I couldn't do that," she replied firmly. "The law is there. Something must happen to it. Imparting birth control information is *not* obscene. If I have done nothing obscene, I cannot plead guilty."

Her supporters, now a steadily growing number, published an open letter to President Wilson. Signed by such intellectual giants as Arnold Bennett and H. G. Wells, it protested the persecution of Margaret Sanger for circulating information on birth control, "which is allowed in every civilized country except the United States." Public sentiment began to snowball in her defense. The night before her trial, a dinner in her honor was given at the Brevoort Hotel, attended by Walter Lippman and other influential liberals. Mary Ware Dennett announced that the National Birth Control League would, after all, stand behind its founder.

Nervous government officials, sensing they had a tiger by the tail in the censorship issue, suddenly decided to drop all charges against Margaret Sanger. She promptly set about confronting them with a new challenge by planning a chain of birth control clinics all over the country, staffed by doctors and nurses "who will instruct women in the things they need to know." Traveling and lecturing in state after state, she organized support for the clinics.

In Portland, Oregon, she was put in jail overnight for distributing copies of *Family Limitation* at a public meeting. Over a hundred women followed her through the streets, insisting that they be jailed along with her.

In the fall of 1916 she organized the first birth control clinic in the United States, violating Section 1142 of the New York Penal Code, which forbade giving contraceptive information to anyone for any reason. She depended for her defense upon Section 1145, which allowed physicians to prescribe anti-conception devices "for the cure or prevention of disease." She intended to broaden this statute, originally designed to protect *men* from venereal disease, to protect women in ill health from excessive child-bearing, and to give them the legal right to avoid this condition.

When her first clinic opened its doors in the poverty-stricken Brownsville area of Brooklyn, New York, over one hundred and fifty shawled, hatless, careworn mothers formed a line halfway to the corner. In their hands they clutched Margaret's leaflet: "MOTHERS! Can you afford to have a large family? Do you want any more children? If not, why do you have them? DO NOT KILL, DO NOT TAKE LIFE, BUT PREVENT. Safe, Harmless Information can be obtained of trained Nurses . . ."

Women began coming from neighboring states as well. One sweatshop worker with eight children pleaded, "If you don't help me, I'll chop up a glass and swallow it tonight!"

After ten days the law had cracked down. Found guilty of violating Section 1142, Margaret Sanger had gone to jail for a month. But she continued writing, lecturing, and crusading until birth control became a popular and respectable topic for public discussion. In 1921, she organized the First National Birth Control Conference, out of which grew a new American Birth Control League. Named its president, Margaret received over a million letters in the next five years from women begging for birth control information.

The League's crusade for changes in the law led to the eventual establishment of Planned Parenthood clinics in almost every state of the union. But it was a hard fight.

Once a district attorney, attempting to smear Margaret as a dangerous subversive, asked her in court if she didn't know anarchist Emma Goldman. "Yes," she admitted blandly, "along with Mrs. Andrew Carnegie and Mrs. John D. Rockefeller." When she signed a contract to lecture in Japan in 1921, the other three lecturers in the group were Albert Einstein, Bertrand Russell, and H. G. Wells.

Despite remarriage to a conservative businessman named J. Noah H. Slee, she continued crusading indefatigably. In 1927, she organized the first World Population Conference at Geneva, where scientists from many nations came together to discuss ways of restricting population to avoid famine.

Margaret Sanger.

When she opened a second Sanger Clinic in New York City in 1929, police raided that one, too. But their seizure of medical records as evidence proved a tactical blunder. The New York County Medical Society angrily protested an obvious violation of the confidential relations between doctor and patient. Police Commissioner Grover Whalen hastily apologized, and a court upheld the right of physicians to prescribe contraception where it "is necessary for a patient's health and physical welfare." Now, at last, public opinion began to swing behind Margaret Sanger.

In March 1931, the Committee on Marriage and the Home of the Federal Council of the Churches of Christ in America approved the desirability of restricting births under medical advice. In November, the American Women's Association awarded Margaret Sanger its medal for "vision, integrity and valor" in her single-handed fight that had "changed the entire social structure of the world."

In 1936, the United States Circuit Court of Appeals upheld the right of doctors in her clinic to import contraception devices, send them through the mail, and prescribe them for patients, "for the purpose of saving life or promoting the well-being of patients." Public approval came from the National Council of Jewish Women, the General Federation of Women's Clubs, the YWCA, local Junior Leagues. In June 1937, the American Medical Association itself came out officially for birth control under medical supervision.

Two years later the Birth Control Federation of America was established, becoming in 1942 the Planned Parenthood Federation of America. Margaret was made first president of the international order organized in 1953, and helped establish population control programs in India and Japan.

Through the door of public acceptance that she opened came another brilliant innovator, Catholic Dr. John Rock, inventor of the birth control pill that is revolutionizing the family science of Planned Parenthood.

Margaret Sanger fought a stubborn, unpopular one-woman crusade against overwhelming odds for a quarter of a century. On September 6, 1966, at the age of eighty-two, she died in Tucson, Arizona, serene in the knowledge that she had helped hundreds of millions of mothers all over the world today to have wanted children, spaced for the best health of mother and child and for the happiness and welfare of the whole family.

14

"The Atomic Clock Ticks Faster"

J. Robert Oppenheimer

A tall, angular man with oddly stiff movements, Dr. J. Robert Oppenheimer, fifty-nine, reported as instructed to the White House on December 7, 1963, to receive the highest honor the US Atomic Energy Commission could bestow—the Enrico Fermi Award. Not pride but the ravages of intense suffering marked his hollowed cheeks, fine nose, and sensitive blue eyes of strange depth and intensity.

His award had been decided upon by President John Kennedy just before his assassination. It was President Lyndon B. Johnson who made the presentation at the White House, as TV cameras flashed to millions of Americans what was in reality a nation's public apology for its ingratitude.

"Dr. Oppenheimer," said the President, "I am pleased that you are here today to receive formal recognition for your many contributions to theoretical physics and to the advancement of science in our nation . . . achievements unique in the scientific world. Even more unique is the demonstration of your scientific and administrative leadership in the forging together of many diverse ideas and experiments in our war effort at Los Alamos and elsewhere."

But only nine years earlier, the Atomic Energy Commission that now bestowed upon him the Fermi Award had branded J. Robert Oppenheimer a security risk because of "fundamental defects" in his character, and had denied him access to secret atomic data he himself had helped discover. In what had amounted to a civilian court-martial, the AEC had disgraced him publicly, making him one of the most reviled and unpopular Americans of the McCarthy era.

President Harry S. Truman once spoke of the nationalistic hysteria that seizes Americans from time to time. He considered rabid anti-Communist emotionalism one of its most insane manifestations. "When we have these fits of hysteria," he sighed, "we are like the person who has a fit of nerves in public—when he recovers, he is very much ashamed—and so are we as a nation when sanity returns."

In 1954 America's sacrificial victim was Oppenheimer.

His father was a successful businessman who had emigrated from Germany at seventeen, his mother an artist and art teacher. Born in New York City in 1904, he was only five when a passionate interest in rocks and minerals whetted his scientific curiosity. Educated at the Ethical Culture School and Harvard, he spent four graduate years abroad studying theoretical physics in England, Germany, and Switzerland.

He returned in 1929 to teach at Berkeley and the California Institute of Technology simultaneously, and was made a full professor at thirty-two. Papers he published in the *Physical Review* on the quantum theory, cosmic rays, and the fundamental particles of nuclear physics won him recognition as a scientific genius. Soon considered one of the world's top ten theoretical physicists, he was welcomed into the group that called itself "the Family." Headed by Niels Bohr, it included Linus Pauling, Leo Szilard, Karl Compton, and Max Born.

Physicists came from all over the world to attend Oppenheimer's seminars and do research under his guidance. Berkeley soon had the outstanding American graduate school in the New Physics. Oppenheimer's disciples were captivated by his charm, eloquence, subtle humor, and brilliant mind, but slow or fuzzy thinkers dreaded his scorn.

Until 1936 he paid little attention to anything but physics. But late that year he found himself becoming deeply disturbed by the state of the world. "I had had a continuing, smoldering fury about the treatment of the Jews in Germany," he explained. "I had relatives there." He was also upset by the effect upon his students of the depression at home.

"Often they could get no jobs, or jobs which were wholly inadequate," he recalled. "And through them I began to understand how deeply political and economic events could affect men's lives. I began to feel the need to participate more fully in the life of the community."

Thousands of intellectuals were joining the Communist Party, among them Oppenheimer's wife, brother, and sister-in-law. Then, in 1936 Franco, with the help of Hitler and Mussolini, attacked the legally elected, democratic Loyalist government of Spain. Hundreds of thousands of outraged Americans joined anti-Fascist organizations, among them Oppenheimer. With the Communists they formed a "United Front" to help Loyalist Spain defeat international Fascism.

In the view of President Eisenhower, Oppenheimer's involvement with the Left had in no way been subversive, but "Dr. Oppenheimer had been guilty of political naiveté."

In August 1939, when Stalin and Hitler signed a non-aggression pact, indicating that Communism had made its peace with Fascism, there was widespread disillusionment on the Left. Oppenheimer dropped out of United Front groups; his wife quit the Communist Party. He was further disillusioned by chilling reports of purges and mismanagement under Stalin from three physicists he met who had worked in the Soviet Union.

His idealism was rekindled when Pearl Harbor brought America into the war against the Axis powers. Eager to make his contribution to help his nation defeat Fascism, he worked on a valuable invention he gave the government to aid plutonium experiments at Oak Ridge. In the spring of 1942, Dr. Arthur Compton, head of scientific research and development for the government, asked him to take charge of building an American atomic bomb. Oppenheimer told him about his former membership in left-wing groups. Compton assured him this would not deny him security clearance for the project.

Gathering about him the top physicists in America, Oppenheimer became the guiding genius of the stupendous research and development at Los Alamos, New Mexico, coordinating the work of forty-five hundred technicians in designing, building, and testing the world's first atomic bomb. All in secret.

He saw no reason to discontinue seeing close personal friends who had been, or still were, Communists or Leftists, like Haakon Chevalier, a French professor at Berkeley. The Soviet Union was now an ally; only Fascism was the enemy. One night at dinner in Oppenheimer's home, Chevalier took him aside to relay a curious message from an English chemical engineer working in Berkeley for Shell Oil, George Eltenton, who had lived in Russia for several years.

Soviet scientists had suggested to Eltenton that closer collaboration between them and United States scientists, with exchanges of atomic information, could benefit their combined war effort against the Germans. So Eltenton had asked Chevalier to sound out Oppenheimer on the idea. Disturbed, Oppenheimer replied that this kind of approach seemed terribly wrong to him. But he assured Chevalier that it had been the proper thing to pass along Eltenton's suggestion.

Months later in 1943, Colonel John Lansdale, security officer for the Manhattan District, told Oppenheimer that he suspected security leaks. Worried, Oppenheimer suggested that Eltenton would bear watching, and told why. But to protect Chevalier, whom he was absolutely sure was innocent, he refused to name him. Instead, he tried to throw intelligence officers off the trail by inventing a story that three Los Alamos bigwigs had been approached, not just himself.

When Oppenheimer's A-bomb was finally perfected, Germany had been knocked out of the war. The dilemma was whether to recommend its use against Japan. "In 1945," recalled Leo Szilard, "when we ceased worrying about what the Germans might do to us, we began to worry about what the government of the United States might do to other countries."

But Oppenheimer, Fermi, Compton, and Lawrence, the interim committee of a scientific panel, recommended that the A-bomb be dropped on Japanese military targets without warning to compel Tokyo to surrender. They were motivated by predictions that the invasion of Japan would cost a million American lives and hoped to avoid that.

The bombs on Hiroshima and Nagasaki did hasten Tokyo's capitulation. Whether their cost in Japanese civilian lives was essential, no one will ever know. On January 12, 1946, President Truman awarded the Medal of Merit to Oppenheimer, declaring, "More than any other one man, Oppenheimer is to be credited with the achievement of the atomic bomb." He cited the scientist's "outstanding service to the War Department, in brilliant accomplishments . . . and his unswerving devotion to duty." Oppenheimer was appointed adviser to the United Nations Atomic Energy Committee Scientific Panel, and also the United States Atomic Energy Commission.

Increasingly uneasy about leaving atomic weapons in the hands of the generals, Oppenheimer urged that they be put under civilian control. He also pleaded for international control of atomic weapons to prevent a terrible atomic arms race. Understandably, these views angered powerful figures in the State Department and the Pentagon. In 1947, as the Cold War grew increasingly bitter, rumors began circulating that Oppenheimer was secretly sympathetic to the Russians.

Dr. James Conant, Director of the National Defense Research Committee, wrote the AEC indignantly, "I can say without hesitation that there can be absolutely no question of Dr. Oppenheimer's loyalty. . . . His attitude about the future course of the United States government in matters of high policy is in accordance with the soundest American tradition." He branded the ugly rumors about Oppenheimer "an absurdity."

Bernard Baruch, the distinguished Chairman of the AEC Advisory Committee, also refuted the slanders, adding, "His is one of the most brilliant minds I have ever encountered."

Oppenheimer refused to make concessions to public opinion shaped by ignorance. He wasn't sleeping well, thinking about the Japanese civilians killed by American A-bombs. "The physicists have known sin," he admitted on November 25, 1947,

President Johnson carries out John F. Kennedy's request that Oppenheimer receive the Enrico Fermi Award for 1963.

"and this is a knowledge which they cannot lose." He urged less atomic secrecy, so that scientists of all nations could cooperate in the use of atomic energy for peaceful purposes.

While serving as scientific adviser to the AEC, he became director of the Institute for Advanced Study in Princeton in 1947. Observed Dr. Hans Bethe, "Oppie made the Institute for Advanced Study *the* place for theoretical physics in the world." Oppenheimer tried to warn Americans that there were no atomic "secrets" from any nation with the physicists and resources to develop A-bombs. Refusing to heed his plea for international control of atomic weapons, Americans were stunned on August 26, 1949, when a mushroom cloud suddenly blossomed up from the wastelands of the Soviet Union.

Oppenheimer pleaded once more for an end to atomic secrecy: "There must be no barriers to freedom of inquiry. There is no place for dogma in science. The scientist is free, and must be free to ask any question, to doubt any assertion." But the alarmed Pentagon pressed for new and bigger secret weapons. When Dr. Edward Teller agreed that it was possible to make a superweapon—the hydrogen bomb—the generals urged that it be developed as quickly as possible to keep an arms race lead.

Oppenheimer objected. The General Advisory Committee to the AEC agreed: "In determining not to proceed to develop the superbomb, we see a unique opportunity of providing by example some limitations on the totality of war and thus of eliminating the fear and arousing the hope of mankind."

Oppenheimer urged instead an all-out United States effort to get the USSR to agree to international control of atomic energy, to prevent a terrible and costly atomic race that might end in a world in flames. His opposition delayed, but did not prevent, development of the H-bomb. He further infuriated the Pentagon and the State Department under John Foster Dulles by a plea in the July 1953 *Bulletin of the Atomic Scientists.*

"The atomic clock ticks faster and faster," he warned. "We may anticipate a state of affairs in which two great powers will each be in a position to put an end to the civilization and life of the other, though not without risking its own. We may be likened to two scorpions in a bottle, each capable of killing the other, but only at the risk of his own life." He ridiculed ignorant bureaucrats who tried to choke off debate because it might reveal vital atomic information to the enemy. "The enemy has this information," he explained. "It is available to anyone who will trouble to make an Intelligence analysis of what has been published."

For fifteen years no one had ever questioned his right to security clearance. Suddenly William L. Borden, a former secretary of the Joint Committee of Congress on Atomic Energy, wrote a letter to the FBI challenging Oppenheimer's access to United States secrets. Borden cited Oppenheimer's opposition to the H-bomb program and his old left-wing associations, declaring, "More probably than not, he has since acted . . . [as] an espionage agent." This letter reached the FBI at the height of the uproar created in Congress by Senator Joseph McCarthy, whose Red hunts were frightening government officials, liberals, and church dignitaries.

"It was a horrible period in American history," said Dr. Henry DeWolf Smyth, United States Ambassador to the International Atomic Energy Commission, "and we paid horribly for it."

The FBI rushed a report on Oppenheimer to Secretary of Defense Charles E. Wilson, who hurried with it to President Eisenhower. Both worried that the Borden accusation would help McCarthy. The President ordered a "blank wall" put between Oppenheimer and classified atomic information. He knew that the scientist had been absolutely loyal, but noted in his diary, "This does not mean that he might not be a security risk." A hearing was arranged.

During April and May 1954, a three-man board headed by university president Gordon Gray listened to the testimony of forty witnesses, which occupies three thousand pages. They dismissed as unimportant Oppenheimer's well-known left-wing ties of the thirties, but denounced the lies he had invented about the Chevalier-Eltenton incident. Asked to explain them, he replied frankly, "I was an idiot." General Leslie R. Groves, head of the atomic program, interpreted them as a "schoolboy" stunt to protect a friend from harassment.

Dr. Vannevar Bush expressed the indignation of both the National Academy of Science and the American Physical Society: "They feel that a professional man who rendered great service to his country . . . beyond almost any other man, is now being pilloried and put through an ordeal because he had the temerity to express his honest opinions. . . . The Republic is in danger today because we have been slipping backward in our maintenance of the Bill of Rights!"

The Gray board of inquiry voted two to one that Oppenheimer was and had been a loyal citizen. But they decided that he was *still* a security risk because of his failure to give "enthusiastic support" to the military's H-bomb program, which had influenced other top scientists against it.

The AEC, ironically, rejected this conclusion, affirming Oppenheimer's right to advise against the development of the H-bomb. But by a four-to-one vote he was condemned as a security risk because of "fundamental defects in his character," as indicated by his lying about the Chevalier incident and by his prewar association with Communists.

His security clearance was revoked, and he was denied access to restricted atomic data. This public stripping of his credentials was enthusiastically approved by Americans who supported Senator McCarthy's policies. In their eyes, Oppenheimer was a traitor for having associated with Communists in the prewar years—before he had even entered upon his distinguished government service.

After reading the hearing testimony, Dr. Walter G. Whitman, Chairman of the Research and Development Board of the Department of Defense, declared, "I do not regard Dr. Oppenheimer as any more of a security risk than I regard myself."

AEC Commissioner Henry DeWolf Smyth, who had disagreed with the majority opinion, blamed Oppenheimer's crucifixion on "enthusiastic help from powerful personal enemies."

Oppenheimer was deeply wounded by the official verdict of the government to which he had given years of his life and his talents. "A less sensitive, a less poetic man could have ignored the trial," declared David Lilienthal, former AEC Chairman. Asked how he felt, Oppenheimer wryly recalled the reply of a soldier asked by a general to describe his role in a great battle: "Sir, I survived."

He persisted in urging an end to the nuclear arms race. "I would like to see a general strike by the officers of all the armed forces on earth," he declared in 1957, "refusing to drop nuclear bombs or to push the fatal button."

Like France's infamous Dreyfus case, the injustice of the Oppenheimer affair deeply troubled the world's intellectuals. Andre Malraux, De Gaulle's brilliant Minister of Culture, felt Oppenheimer had made a mistake in playing his accusers' game. "He should categorically have refused to answer questions about the political opinions or associations or affiliations of his friends and associates," Malraux declared. "He should have stood on the ground that he was the builder of the atom bomb—a scientist, not an informer."

Dr. Max Born, teacher of the world's leading atomic physicists, said sadly, "Oppenheimer tried to resist the production of the hydrogen bomb, but . . . he was squeezed out of the Atomic Energy Commission of the American government."

Dr. Ward V. Evans, the Gray board's dissenting member, had warned, "Our failure to clear Dr. Oppenheimer will be a black mark on the escutcheon of our country." Finally, in 1963, a shamefaced Atomic Energy Commission decided that Evans was right and tried to make amends to J. Robert Oppenheimer by presenting him with the Fermi Award.

A few months before his death, Oppenheimer was asked when he thought the international nuclear arms race might end. "When the nuclear 'haves' agree to disarm their arsenals," he replied. "This will affect how the nuclear 'have-nots' act. They may not try to fight their way into the nuclear club if we voluntarily come out."

He died on February 25, 1967—the same year that saw the United States and the USSR finally reach preliminary agreements on international nuclear arms control and the banning of nuclear weapons in outer space.

Upon news of his death, the Board of Governors of the International Atomic Energy Agency, representing twenty-five nations of the world, interrupted their deliberations to pay tribute to the scientific achievements of J. Robert Oppenheimer and his lonely fight to protect the world from nuclear bombs.

In America Dr. DeWolf Smyth said, "We share Oppenheimer's deep regret that a brilliant discovery of science had to be perverted to an appalling weapon. We regret that his great work for his country was repaid so shabbily. . . . If he paid heavily, as indeed he did, we hope he knew how greatly his country and the world have been rewarded by his work."

But perhaps the finest tribute to Oppenheimer was paid him by the same President under whose administration he had been disgraced in the eyes of Americans.

"Here in America," said Dwight D. Eisenhower on June 10, 1954, "we are descended in blood and spirit from revolutionaries and rebels—men and women who dared to dissent from accepted doctrines. As their heirs, may we never confuse honest dissent with disloyal subversion."

15

"My God, I Feel So Alone!"

J. William Fulbright

He was heartily disliked by his former friend, President Lyndon B. Johnson. He was unpopular with the State Department, the Pentagon, the CIA, and defense contractors with war contracts. He was fiercely hated by ultrarightist groups, who excoriated him as "freedom's Judas-goat."

The man described by the *New York Times* as "the conscience of American foreign policy" was a mild-mannered, thoughtful, courteous, soft-voiced former college professor turned politician—Senator J. William Fulbright of Arkansas, Chairman of the powerful Senate Foreign Relations Committee since 1959, the voice of Americans who opposed an expansionist United States foreign policy.

As Fulbright saw it, "The idea of being responsible for the whole world seems to be flattering to Americans, and I am afraid it is turning our heads, just as the sense of global responsibility turned the heads of ancient Romans and nineteenth century British . . . dangerous nonsense in this age of nuclear weapons." He believed that a Cold War fixation led Washington away from the path of reason, blundering into mistakes that alienated world opinion.

"The role he plays in Washington is an indispensable role," observed Walter Lippman. "There is no one else so powerful and also so wise. Not only has he been the bravest and wisest of advisers. He is also the most farseeing and constructive." President John Kennedy had wanted to make him Secretary of State but Fulbright refused, feeling this role would chain him to government policy as an apologist.

No wild radical, he was conservative, aristocratic, reflective, shunning crowds and emotional scenes. He would often stay up until 2 a.m. absorbed in a study of Chinese history. A highly complex man, he was in turn witty, erudite, earthy, sardonic, melancholy, shrewd, and naïve. The quiet courage of his convictions often led him to point out what everyone else was afraid to—that the emperor who thought he was garbed in the finest raiment was actually naked.

He was born on a Missouri farm on April 9, 1905, the fourth of six children. His father was a quiet, hardworking corn-hog farmer who moved to Fayetteville, Arkansas, in 1906, started a small business, and died in 1924 owning most of the town. His mother was a political liberal who wrote a newspaper column and taught at the University of Arkansas.

As a boy, young Fulbright preferred the company of his own thoughts as he hiked and rode horseback through the mountains of Arkansas. He was only sixteen when he entered the University as a political-science major. Organizing a student government, he was elected its president. A quiet intellectual who rarely volunteered answers, he preferred asking shrewd questions that exposed the weakness of any argument. "It wasn't very smart to argue with him," one professor recalled.

He was the University's star halfback for three and a half years, winning national sports fame by an uncanny knack of finding holes in the rival line and plunging through. It was a knack he later adapted to politics with devastating effect. A Rhodes scholarship took him to England for three years. As "an Ozark hillbilly at Oxford," he learned to be skeptical of all political dogma; travels around Europe gave him a sophisticated, international viewpoint.

Returning home, he won a law degree from George Washington University Law School, worked briefly for the Department of Justice, then taught law for four years. In 1939, at the age of only thirty-four, the University of Arkansas appointed him its president. But two years later he was fired when his mother antagonized Homer Adkins, the new Governor, by describing him in her column as a "handshaking, backslapping politician."

He reluctantly agreed to run for Congress in 1942 when one of his former pupils turned Congressman reminded him about his lectures on the need for educated men in politics.

Winning a seat in the House of Representatives, he sought and was given a place on the Foreign Affairs Committee. His brilliance was quickly apparent when, as a freshman Congressman, he led the United States out of its isolationism into a commitment to join a postwar world organization to enforce peace. In September 1943, the House passed the Fulbright Concurrent Resolution to this effect 360 to 29, and six weeks later the Senate concurred. J. William Fulbright had opened the door to the creation of the United Nations.

In 1944, with America swept by war fervor, Fulbright campaigned for the Senate by reminding Arkansas voters that even though the fight against Fascism was a just war, warfare itself was a tragedy to grieve thoughtful men: "I hate war, not only because it destroys our young men, our families, our property, but because it will sooner or later destroy our system of free enterprise. War will inevitably make us slaves of an organized bureaucracy, and this would happen whether we won or lost. The democratic system . . . is not designed for war." He won the Senate seat handily, defeating the same Governor Homer Adkins who had had him fired as university president.

When Roosevelt's death in 1945 made Harry S. Truman President, Fulbright went to the White House to see whether Truman felt committed to postwar world peace. He was dismayed to find the new President a strong nationalist who believed in relying on military power, not the United Nations.

"I didn't make a bit of impression on him," Fulbright sighed later. "He didn't know what I was talking about."

In his first Senate speech on March 28, 1945, Fulbright warned against a postwar anti-Russian policy that would inflame Soviet suspicions of American intentions. He reminded Senators that in 1918 the United States had sent an armed expedition against the Soviet Union without provocation, and had refused to recognize the Soviet government until 1933.

"Since we have been the most successful revolutionary people in history," he asked, "why are we so critical of others who follow our example?" He added, "I realize that it is not popular to compare Russia with ourselves, and yet it is necessary to get our ideas straight. When I hear the unbridled and intemperate attacks upon Russia by some of our people, I cannot help but be troubled. . . . We must demonstrate the superiority of individual initiative under capitalism by our results, by the provision of a superior way of life, not by the violence of our oratory."

He watched in dismay as the United Nations was weakened by the Cold War between its two most powerful members. He deplored Stalin's aggressive postwar moves in Eastern Europe, but felt they had been provoked in part by the United States' refusal to permit adequate German reparations for Nazi destruction in Russia, and denial to the USSR of either warm water ports or a share of Middle East oil. When Washington protested against Soviet military bases in eastern Europe, Moscow simply pointed to strategic American bases in the Pacific. Fulbright urged placing our Pacific bases under United Nations trusteeship so we could then challenge the USSR to do the same.

Truman and the State Department ignored him coldly.

Deeply worried about a United States-USSR clash that could bring on a disastrous World War III, Fulbright questioned Dr. J. Robert Oppenheimer at Senate hearings in September 1945 to make Americans realize that there was no such thing as atomic "secrets"; that it would be only five years or less before the USSR and other nations had their own atomic bombs.

"We are the only people who can make atom bombs," replied President Truman tartly, "and we'll keep it that way!" But in 1949 he was forced to admit, "We have evidence that within recent weeks an atomic explosion occurred in the USSR." Few Americans remembered that on November 23, 1945, Fulbright had predicted it, protesting, "The President professes a faith in the United Nations, but . . . we keep the atomic bomb to ourselves under the guise of a self-appointed sacred trusteeship." Now the deadly arms race was on.

When Oppenheimer was branded a security risk for opposing development of the H-bomb as just "more of same," Fulbright said sadly, "This is but the latest chapter in the development of anti-intellectualism . . . throughout the country."

He had done everything he could think of to develop a greater sophistication in American thinking, including helping more bright young Americans—future molders of United States opinion—develop the international insights that had been his privilege as a Rhodes scholar. In 1945 he had developed a plan to sell surplus war property abroad, using the funds in the countries where it was sold to pay for tuition, books, and living expenses of American exchange students and teachers, as well as for the future leaders of those countries to come to the United States to study. The Fulbright Scholarship Act had, in two decades, provided almost a hundred thousand opportunities for bright Americans to train abroad in the arts and sciences, and the educated elite of foreign nations to learn about and take home a better understanding of the United States.

President Kennedy described Fulbright scholarships as "the classic modern example of beating swords into ploughshares." Even Fulbright's dogged enemy, the State Department, admitted that they were "the most fabulously profitable investment ever authorized by Congress." His former history tutor at Oxford told him, "You are responsible for the largest and most significant movement of scholars across the face of the earth since the fall of Constantinople in 1453."

The Cold War and the arms race inspired a climate of fear in the United States that demagogues were not slow to take advantage of for their own political ambitions. No American phenomenon appalled Fulbright more than the emergence of Senator Joseph McCarthy as spokesman for the extreme Right and the politically illiterate. He referred to "this swinish blight" known as "McCarthyism."

But in January 1954, the Gallup Poll showed that 50 percent of the American people, worried about Communism, generally approved of the junior Senator from Wisconsin.

McCarthy's wild accusations against Eisenhower, all Democrats, and the State Department filled public figures, educators, and scientists with a dread of the label "Commie."

"Some of the best minds in the land were expelled from government service," Fulbright later said, "and a suspicion of educated people was spread through the land as if they were enemy aliens."

As chairman of a Senate subcommittee, McCarthy used his powers to win sensational headlines with one-sided hearings at which he hurled Communist charges at government officials and agencies. When the Senate Foreign Relations Committee met to consider the appointment of an Eisenhower nominee, McCarthy testified against his confirmation. He threatened members of the Committee with political defeat if they dared vote to confirm the nominee over his opposition.

"This is perfectly ridiculous," Fulbright declared in disgust. "Are all his cases just as ridiculous? . . . Never have I seen a more arrogant or rude witness before a committee!" McCarthy's supporters filled his mail with obscene attacks. Some of the milder samples: "You have been a party to the Roosevelt-Truman-

Acheson-Hiss gang of traitors for 20 years." . . . "A fine dirty red rat are you." . . . "I would spit on you!" Fulbright told the Senate sadly, "I think they evidence a great sickness among our people."

He understood McCarthy's motives even if millions of Americans didn't. "There was a certain method to this madness," he explained, "for if every corner of our society could be made to appear a nest of treason, then the way would be open for McCarthyism to make its supreme bid for naked power—all in the name of purifying the social order."

In 1954, McCarthy had so intimidated the nation's lawmakers that only Fulbright dared vote against an appropriation of $214,000 for his subcommittee. "I don't see why I should buy a gun for the man to shoot decent citizens with," he declared. He told a University of Minnesota audience, "If we had not neglected the education of our citizens, I do not believe we would be witnessing this phenomenon today. . . . Do you believe if the people of Wisconsin—or even the members of the Senate—thoroughly understood the lessons of Hitler, Mussolini, and Stalin, that we would permit the trifling with our basic institutions and our liberties that has been going on for months?" In McCarthy territory, that took courage.

McCarthy finally blundered by agreeing to televised hearings of his alleged Red spy plot within the Army. TV broadcasts gave Americans a firsthand look at a McCarthy witch hunt, and they were stunned by what they saw. National revulsion set in. The Senate now eagerly welcomed a censure resolution against McCarthy brought by Senators Fulbright, Ralph Flanders of Vermont, and Wayne Morse of Oregon, for bringing discredit upon the Senate by his obnoxious behavior. The Senate voted for censure 67 to 22. President Eisenhower called it "a splendid job." McCarthy's political power was smashed.

Why had he been able to establish a reign of terror? Because, Fulbright explained, the United States government and press had made rigid anti-Communism into a national religion "unpatriotic" to question. Americans had not been encouraged to consider other ways to meet the Communist challenge except witch hunts at home and saber rattling abroad. To be free of the suspicion of being a "Commie," a public official had to join those stampeding the public with loud cries of alarm about the Red menace.

A public servant who dared point out the alternatives, Fulbright said on January 25, 1955, "must be prepared to accept banishment or destruction at the hands of the people because he has aroused their anger in the very act of serving them well." He continued to point out the alternatives.

He was distinctly unhappy with Eisenhower's Secretary of State, John Foster Dulles, whose program of militarism, Fulbright said, appealed to "unthinking people." He was outraged when Dulles, after obvious failures of his Middle East policy, testified before the Foreign Relations Committee in 1956 that it was succeeding. Fulbright's sardonic questioning made Dulles squirm with embarrassment.

"Is the government well served," Fulbright drawled, "when a Secretary of State misleads public opinion, confuses it, feeds it pap, tells it that . . . Soviet triumphs are really defeats, and Western defeats are really triumphs?"

He warned Dulles against sending arms to Pakistan in 1956: "By pouring in great quantities of arms we create local problems that may cause an immediate outbreak of hostilities." Nine years later, twelve thousand troops were killed by United States arms supplied to both Pakistan and India in battles over Kashmir. The Soviet Union scored a diplomatic victory by arranging peace at Tashkent in a war fought with Dulles's arms shipments.

On June 20, 1958, Fulbright warned, "We now have approximately 275 major [military] base complexes . . . in 31 countries. . . . These bases must certainly also provoke the Russians. Have we understood that fact? . . . We have treated constant Soviet preoccupation with our overseas bases as a sort of

Joseph McCarthy testifies about Communist activities at hearings in 1954, while Joseph N. Welch, the Army counsel, sits dejectedly.

unreasonable Soviet obsession. Speaking for myself, I am frank to admit that I might find myself plagued by an obsession against Soviet bases if their ballistic-launching facilities were in the Caribbean or Mexico."

Four years later, Americans were stunned and brought to the brink of nuclear war when the Soviet Union finally did establish a military base in Cuba at Castro's invitation. They had forgotten that in 1958 Fulbright had urged disarmament talks with the USSR before both countries were forced into a nuclear confrontation neither wanted.

He had also asked, "Is anyone in this chamber prepared to say, for example, that war has become an impossibility between Israel and the Arab states?" Nine years later the Arab-Israeli War had broken out, frightening the world until the United States and the USSR both hastily reassured each other that they would not be dragged into it.

Fulbright grew increasingly disgusted with Dulles's policy of promising money, arms, and United States troops to any country that, threatened by internal revolution, professed to be attacked by Communist forces from outside. This Eisenhower Doctrine led to the sending of United States Marines into Lebanon in 1958 to crush a domestic uprising that United Nations observers certified as a civil war. Fulbright charged angrily, "Our foreign policy is inadequate, outmoded, and misdirected. . . . If we go on as we are, soon—in the fashion of the cat on the hot tin roof—we shall be skipping from one crisis to another all over the globe, unable to get our footing anywhere."

He warned against the United States policy of propping up unpopular right-wing governments with American arms. United States arms given to Chiang Kai-shek, he pointed out, had been captured by Red China and used to kill Americans in Korea. "Will we never learn, Mr. President?" he demanded. "How many more Americans must be killed by our foolish gifts of weapons to shaky governments before we learn?" He urged an end to the "devil theory"—the claim that anytime our policies failed, "we have a ready answer: the Soviet Union is behind it. What a perfect formula for the evasion of reality!"

Fulbright was made Chairman of the Senate Foreign Relations Committee on January 30, 1959. He announced, as the cornerstone of his political thinking, a conviction that the United States and the USSR had to learn to coexist in the same world. He prophesied that in time world opinion would compel the Soviet Union to ease its control of eastern Europe. "We may even hope," he said, "that, as conditions of life improve in the USSR, the harsh and brutal attitude of the Russians toward their fellow men may be humanized." The speech strongly impressed the new Soviet Premier, Nikita Khrushchev, who not only condemned the crimes of Stalin, but proposed his own belief in the necessity of a coexistence policy.

In 1960 Khrushchev paid a goodwill visit to the United States, leading to the calling of a summit conference in Paris. But when an American U-2 plane spying for the CIA was forced down over Russia on the eve of the conference, Khrushchev demanded a United States apology and a promise to end such espionage. Eisenhower not only refused, but took personal responsibility for the U-2 incident. Khrushchev then stormed out of the conference, chilling world hopes for an East-West treaty to end the Cold War. Fulbright demanded an inquiry into the U-2 fiasco.

"Suppose a Russian counterpart of the U-2 had come down over Kansas City on May 1," he pointed out. "This event in itself would have brought speeches in the Senate powerful enough to rock the Capitol dome with denunciations of the perfidy of the Soviets on the eve of the summit conference. . . . Then reflect how much more violent the reaction here would have been if Mr. Khrushchev had said he was personally responsible . . . [with] every intention of trying it again."

Fulbright demanded closer Congressional control over the CIA to stop its usurpation of the role of making foreign policy. Senator John Kennedy agreed with Fulbright that America owed an apology for violating international law.

In 1961, Fulbright learned that the National Defense Council was allowing generals in uniform to take part in extremist political meetings to propagandize for the Cold War and indoctrinate troops with a right-wing viewpoint. He protested to the Secretary of Defense, "There has been a strong tradition in this country that it is not the function of the military to educate the public on political issues." President Kennedy supported Fulbright, ordering the Armed Forces to stop using the uniform to interfere in politics.

Enraged at Fulbright, the radical Right raised a huge campaign fund to defeat him at the next election. They told Arkansas voters, "Your representative has voted 89 percent of the time to aid and abet the Communist Party!" In his campaign for reelection, Fulbright mocked the Right's obsession with seeing Reds everywhere. "Now, you know that's nonsense," he scoffed to his constituents. "How many Communists do you know at the Courthouse? Or among your teachers? Or preachers? . . . Internal Communism is a very minor problem with us, and one I think the FBI can handle quite well."

The voters of Arkansas sent him back to the Senate with an overwhelming majority in every county but one.

Fulbright was shocked when he learned about the CIA's plan to invade Cuba and overthrow Castro with a force of Cuban exiles trained, financed, and armed by the United States. He warned President Kennedy that the whole idea was "an endless can of worms" that was bound to backfire badly. Its success was dubious, might compel open United States intervention, and was bound to provoke angry Latin-American cries of *"Imperialismo Yanqui."* But when Kennedy called a meeting of top advisers at the State Department on April 4, 1962, Fulbright's was the lone voice to speak out against the CIA plot.

"The Castro regime is a thorn in the flesh," he admitted, "but it is not a dagger in the heart." He also cautioned, "I have no evidence that the Cuban people are able and willing at this time to assist any invasion from the outside." But Kennedy, unsure of himself, felt compelled to trust the CIA scheme worked out under Eisenhower, which had the unanimous support of all Kennedy's advisers.

When the Bay of Pigs invasion turned out to be the horrible fiasco Fulbright had predicted, Kennedy asked, "How could I have agreed to such a stupid mistake?" At a gloomy gathering of his advisers at the White House, he admitted to Fulbright, "You are the only person here who has a right to say: 'I told you so!'" The Bay of Pigs blunder not only crippled United States prestige in the eyes of the world, but drove Castro to turn to the USSR for protection. The installation of Soviet missile bases in Cuba then brought on the Kennedy-Khrushchev "eyeball-to-eyeball" confrontation that alarmed the whole world—until Khrushchev averted a nuclear war by agreeing to dismantle the Soviet missile bases.

When Kennedy's assassination made Lyndon Johnson President, Fulbright was eager to support what he hoped would finally be a new liberal direction for United States foreign policy. But he grew more and more discouraged as American involvement in the Vietnam War grew deeper and deeper. When three enemy torpedo boats exchanged fire with a United States destroyer in the Gulf of Tonkin, President Johnson went to Congress on August 6, 1964, and asked for a resolution authorizing him "to take all necessary measures . . . to prevent further aggression." Fulbright hesitantly agreed to co-sponsor the resolution, and voted for it.

Using this resolution as a mandate, the Johnson Administration escalated the undeclared Vietnam War from the use of a few thousand United States troops as advisers to the South Vietnam Army to an American war fought by half a million United States troops with United States planes bombing North Vietnam. Never before in American history were Americans so divided and doubtful about the wisdom or justice of a war fought by the United States.

Fulbright's growing alarm about American foreign policy reached a climax in spring 1965, when civil war against a three-man ruling military junta broke out in the Dominican Republic. Supporters of the mildly left-wing Juan Bosch, who had been elected President legally by the Dominican people before being overthrown by the junta's coup, were leading the revolt. United States troops were rushed in. At first it was said that their purpose was to protect the safety of American personnel in the Dominican Republic. But TV news films showed United States troops aiding the military junta.

The Administration then changed its story, saying that Communists had taken over the revolt. Investigating, Fulbright found no evidence of this claim, but so much falsification by the CIA and the Administration that he was dismayed. The press began to talk about the Administration's "credibility gap"—that is, its lack of believability.

Knowing it would cost him his personal friendship with the President, Fulbright held Foreign Relations Committee hearings behind closed doors. Afterward, he charged that the Dominican intervention had been a panicky mistake by the Administration. "United States policy was marred by a lack of candor and by misinformation. . . . The danger to American lives was more a pretext than a reason for the massive United States intervention." He cited a second blunder in the failure to consult with the Organization of American States first.

Enraged at Fulbright, the Administration struck back by steamrollering a resolution through the House, 315 to 52, endorsing the right of the United States to use force anywhere to prevent a Communist takeover. Administration supporters sharply criticized Fulbright for refusing to back the President.

His defense came from Republican Senator Margaret Chase Smith: "I not only defend his right to express his deeply felt views and his sharp dissent; I admire him for speaking his mind and his conscience. I admire him for his courage to run counter to conformity and the overwhelming majority."

American doubts over the United States involvement in Vietnam rose sharply after the Dominican misadventure. The World Council of Churches and the academic community now shared Fulbright's misgivings about the drift of foreign policy.

The basic disagreement between Fulbright and the Johnson Administration over Vietnam lay in their different concepts of the basic nature of the conflict. The Administration saw the war as resulting from the invasion of South Vietnam by North Vietnam, led by Communist Ho Chi Minh and instigated by Red China, in a drive to Communize all of Southeast Asia. At first the United States had sent aid and advisers to the shaky, unpopular South Vietnam government. When the South Vietnamese had proved corrupt, inefficient, and unwilling to fight, the United States had sent its own troops to prosecute the war.

Fulbright saw the war as basically a civil war between Vietnam Communists—Vietcong in South Vietnam supported by Ho Chi Minh's Communist forces in the North—and the Saigon military dictatorship of South Vietnam, which represented the Army and the rich landlords opposed to land reform. They had come to power with United States support when the French, who had previously held Vietnam as a colony, were defeated and forced out by Ho Chi Minh.

A Geneva peace treaty had temporarily divided the country in half in 1954, with elections scheduled for two years later to decide a new government for all Vietnam. John Foster Dulles, who knew that Ho Chi Minh, as the "George Washington" of the Vietnamese, would be elected President, saw to it that a non-Communist government in South Vietnam prevented the election. (President Eisenhower himself admitted that 80 percent of all Vietnamese would have voted for Ho Chi Minh.)

Senator Fulbright poses a question during a session of the Senate Foreign Relations Committee discussion of Vietnam.

Fulbright saw Dulles's interference in the Geneva settlement, and his support for a South Vietnam government in opposition to Ho Chi Minh, as the basic error that had plunged the United States into deep trouble. In the eyes of Fulbright and most nations of the world, the United States had interfered in a civil war and was preventing a nationalistic, unified Vietnam because it would be Communist.

Fulbright tried to convince President Johnson that the United States was mistaken in its Vietnam policy, but admitted afterward, "He was not persuaded." The President was convinced by the Pentagon and the State Department that Ho Chi Minh was a pawn of Red China and had to be stopped to stop Red Chinese expansion. He accepted the theory that heavy United States bombing of North Vietnam would compel Ho Chi Minh to stop supporting the Vietcong in South Vietnam, and make permanent the division of North and South Vietnam.

But Fulbright was increasingly upset by the cost of this policy in American lives. He recalled that President Kennedy, discussing the South Vietnamese in September 1963, had declared, "In the final analysis, it's their war. They're the ones who have to win it or lose it. We can help, give them equipment, we can send our men out there as advisers, but they have to win it."

The Johnson Administration, Fulbright felt, had reversed that view, turning Vietnam into a war fought almost entirely by American troops—almost half a million by 1967. Like increasing numbers of Americans on the home front, Fulbright was sickened by the savagery of the war. There were atrocities on both sides. The Vietcong abducted and murdered civilians and committed acts of terror. South Vietnamese troops tortured Vietcong prisoners. United States troops used napalm bombs against native men, women, and children.

Horrified world opinion demanded an end to the war.

As hundreds of American deaths in the war turned to thousands, Fulbright was shocked by evidence that the Administration had turned a deaf ear to peace feelers from Hanoi. On November 21, 1965, he said to Senator Vance Hartke, "My God, I feel so alone! I feel at times that I am walking among the blind and the deaf!" He decided that the time had come to open up a public debate on Vietnam.

It began on January 28, 1966, with a Senate Foreign Relations Committee hearing on the Administration request for an extra $275 million in aid for South Vietnam. From then until spring, the American people watching on TV heard the questing intellect of J. William Fulbright by his brilliant cross-examination of uncomfortable Administration spokesmen, encourage them to think "unthinkable thoughts."

He introduced them to experts like General James Gavin and ex-Ambassador George Kennan, who firmly opposed the Administration's escalation of the war. The hearings led new millions of Americans to protest United States foreign policy.

During March and April, there were tremendous antiwar demonstrations, parades, and rallies all over the country. The World Council of Churches, in opposition to State Department policy, demanded direct negotiations with the Vietcong.

His temerity in airing open criticism of the Administration's Vietnam policy understandably brought blasts against Fulbright from Democratic Party wheel horses.

"I believe," he replied firmly, "that the citizen who criticizes his country is paying it an implied tribute. . . . It means that he has not given up on his country, that he still has hope for it. . . . I do not think it is 'selling America short' when we ask a great deal of her; on the contrary, it is those who ask nothing, those who see no fault, who are really selling America short!"

But when the Administration showed no sign of heeding his warnings, he sighed wearily, "I feel so isolated and discouraged. Good God, I'm discouraged! The war fever is increasing. We Americans are so powerful and so self-righteous!"

On May 25 he invited two leading psychiatrists to the Senate hearings. They testified that from a psychiatric point of view, the Cold War "psychosis" was a sickness that had developed into "national schizophrenia"—seeing oneself as a noble, innocent victim against whom evil forces everywhere are plotting. The diagnosis, they explained, fitted the foreign policy of three major powers: Red China. The USSR. And the United States.

Fulbright urged the American people not to fall victim to "the arrogance of power." The real answer to dealing with Red China, he advised, was not a Vietnam War but to end China's isolation from the West with trade and scientific and cultural exchanges, as we were doing with the Communist nations of eastern Europe. He urged sincere efforts to end the Vietnam War, assuring Americans that the United States was great and powerful enough to make amends for its mistakes without suffering any loss of world prestige.

The *Manchester Guardian,* one of Britain's most influential newspapers, saw a moral victory for Fulbright over the Administration. "The turning point came," it editorialized, "with the hearings of the Senate Foreign Relations Committee, and Senator Fulbright, the hero of those encounters."

But the President angrily attacked "nervous Nellies" who were "ready to turn on their own leaders, their own country, and their own fighting men." He summoned Fulbright to the White House to try to talk him into support of the war. Fulbright raised objection after objection, but found that the President would not listen. "The President is all wrapped up in a religious war," he concluded gloomily.

Fulbright remained convinced that the United States made a fatal blunder in trying to play policeman to the world instead of strengthening the United Nations to do this vital job.

He further believed that it was shortsighted for the United States to give direct foreign aid to other countries, particularly when they were governed by unpopular dictatorships, and then feel obligated to back them up militarily when they were threatened with overthrow by their own people. "The Vietnam War began as a foreign aid program," he warned. He would have liked to see American foreign aid channeled through an international agency like the United Nations or the World Bank.

If Fulbright was an expert at pointing out the Achilles' heel of Presidents, he was not without one of his own. Unlike most intellectuals, he was conservative on civil rights.

"My constituents have rather strong feelings on this subject," he once said candidly, "and since they permit me a great deal of freedom in foreign policy, I think I should respect their wishes." He bluntly admitted to one reporter, "I can't vote my own convictions on civil rights. If I did, I wouldn't be returned to the Senate. It's as simple as that." Few Negro leaders are impressed by this explanation.

But J. William Fulbright continued to be the spokesman of Americans disenchanted with United States foreign policy. He ironically retitled the Great Society promised by President Johnson the Sick Society. Taken to task for "letting our boys down in Vietnam," Fulbright replied quietly, "They didn't ask to go there. They were ordered there. I would think the best we could do for them would be to work very hard for an honorable peace."

Still very much the professor under his Senatorial toga, he hoped eventually to educate Americans into relinquishing their McCarthy-Dulles view of the world as an outmoded "mythology." Our foreign policy troubles, he was convinced, wouldn't end until we realized that the Cold War situations of the late forties and the fifties lost all relevance in the changing world picture.

"Are we to be the friend or the enemy of the social revolutions of Asia and Latin America?" he asked in a speech at Storrs University. If we do not want the Communist Revolution to inspire them, he pointed out, then we must let the successful American

Revolution be "an example for those around the world who seek freedom."

Since World War II, the courageous Senator from Arkansas, almost single-handedly challenged majority opinion in the United States and waited patiently for the American people to come around to his often unpopular views. He had an astonishing record of proving to be right about many tragic blunders of American foreign policy he warned against.

Like Thoreau and the other Unpopular Ones of America, courage and integrity forced J. William Fulbright to march to the sound of a different drummer—out of step with his day, in step with the future.

ABOUT THE AUTHOR

Jules Archer was one of the most respected names in nonfiction for young people. During his lifetime he published over seventy books, which have been translated into twelve languages throughout the world. He lived in Scotts Valley, California, until his death in 2008.

Bibliography

Andrews, John. *History of the War With America, France and Spain.* 4 vols. London: John Fielding and John Jarvis, 1785.

Archer, Jules. *Battlefield President: Dwight D. Eisenhower.* New York: Julian Messner, 1967.

_____. *Fighting Journalist: Horace Greeley.* New York: Julian Messner, 1966.

_____. *World Citizen: Woodrow Wilson.* New York: Julian Messner, 1967.

Belcher, Henry. *The First American Civil War.* London: Macmillan and Co., Ltd., 1911.

Brierly, J. Ernest. *The Streets of Old New York.* New York: Hastings House, 1953.

Buranelli, Vincent. *The Trial of Peter Zenger.* New York: New York University Press, 1957.

Chaplin, J. P. *Rumor, Fear and the Madness of Crowds.* New York: Ballantine Books, 1959.

Chevalier, Haakon. *Oppenheimer: The Story of a Friendship.* New York: George Braziller, 1965.

Chute, William J., ed. *The American Scene: 1860 to the Present.* New York, Toronto, London: Bantam Books, 1966.

Coffin, Tristam. *Senator Fulbright: Portrait of a Public Philosopher.* New York: E. P. Dutton & Co., 1966.

Curtis, Charles P. *The Oppenheimer Case.* New York: Simon & Schuster, 1955.

Derleth, August. *Concord Rebel: A Life of Henry D. Thoreau.* Philadelphia and New York: Chilton Company, 1962.

Ditzion, Sidney. *Marriage, Morals and Sex in America.* New York: Bookman Associates, 1953.

Fulbright, J. William. *A Legislator's Thoughts on World Issues.* New York: Macfadden Books, 1964.

Gordon, William. *The History of the Rise, Progress and Establishment of the United States of America.* 4 vols. London: Charles Dilly and James Buckland, 1788.

Grigson, Geoffrey, and Charles Harvard Gibbs-Smith, eds. *People.* New York: Hawthorn Books, [[1957]].

Grodzins, Morton, and Eugene Rabinowitch, eds. *The Atomic Age.* New York, London: Basic Books, 1963.

Gurko, Leo. *Tom Paine: Freedom's Apostle.* New York: Thomas Y. Crowell Company, 1957.

Holbrook, Stewart H. *Dreamers of the American Dream.* Garden City, New York: Doubleday & Company, 1957.

————. *Lost Men of American History.* New York: The Macmillan Company, 1946.

Lader, Lawrence. *The Bold Brahmins.* New York: E. P. Dutton & Co., 1961.

Lehmann-Russbuldt, Otto. *War For Profits.* New York: Alfred H. King, 1930.

McPharlin, Paul. *Life and Fashion in America, 1650–1900.* New York: Hastings House, 1946.

Morgan, H. Wayne. *Eugene V. Debs: Socialist for President.* Syracuse, New York: Syracuse University Press, 1962.

Pierson, George Wilson. *Tocqueville in America.* Garden City, New York: Doubleday & Company, 1959.

Porter, Sarah Harvey. *The Life and Times of Anne Royall.* Cedar Rapids, Iowa: The Torch Press Book Shop, 1909.

Riegel, Robert E. *American Feminists.* Lawrence, Kansas: University of Kansas Press, 1963.

Rutherford, Livingston. *John Peter Zenger.* New York: Peter Smith, 1941.

Sanger, Margaret. *Margaret Sanger: An Autobiography.* New York: W. W. Norton & Company, 1938.

Siebert, Wilbur H. *The Underground Railroad From Slavery to Freedom.* New York, London: The Macmillan Company, 1898.

Thomas, John L. *The Catholic Viewpoint on Marriage and the Family.* Garden City, New York: Hanover House, 1958.

Truman, Harry S. *Memoirs.* New York: New American Library, 1965.

Wallace, Irving. *The Square Pegs.* New York: Alfred A. Knopf, 1957.

Whittier, John Greenleaf. *The Poetical Works of John Greenleaf Whittier.* Boston: Fields, Osgood & Co., 1870.

Whitton, Mary Ormsbee. *These Were the Women.* New York: Hastings House, 1954.

Woodward, William E. *The Way Our People Lived.* New York: Washington Square Press, 1965.

Wise, David, and Thomas B. Ross. *The Invisible Government.* New York, Toronto, London: Bantam Books, 1965.

Index

A Week on the Concord and Merrimack Rivers, 70
Acheson, Dean, 163
Adair, Col. John, 129
Adams, John Quincy, 23, 36, 38, 42, 45
Adamson Act, 104
Adkins, Governor Homer, 159
Age of Reason, The, 29
Alcott, Bronson, 51
Allen, Ethan, 45
Altgeld, Governor of Illinois, 99
American Asylum for the Deaf and Dumb, 37
American Civil Liberties Union, 52
American Federation of Labor, 101
American Medical Association, 130, 142
American Physical Society, 153
American Railway Union, 97
American Women's Association, 142
Anthony, Susan B., 89, 90
Anti-Vietnam protests, 77
Appeal to Reason, 100
Arab-Israeli War, 165
Arms Control, 155
Army-McCarthy Hearings, 163, 165
Arnold, Benedict, xiv

Baez, Joan, 72
Barnum, P. T., 65, 89

Baruch, Bernard, 150
Bay of Pigs invasion, 168
Beaumont, Gustave de, 87
Beecher, Henry Ward, 60
Bellows (jailer), 49–51
Bennett, Arnold, 139
Bennett, James Gordon, 87
Bethe, Dr. Hans, 151
Bigelow, John, 65
Birth control, 131–143
Bloody Tenent, The, 7–9
Bloomer, Amelia, 85–93
Bloomer, Dexter C., 86, 87, 88, 92
Bohr, Niels, 146
Borah, Senator William, 116
Borden, William L., 152
Born, Max, 146, 154
Bosch, Juan, 169
Bradford, William, 12, 14
Branded Hand, The, 83
Brigham, Justice, 48, 50, 51
Brisbane, Arthur, 59
Brown, John, 62, 75, 76
Brown, Antoinette, 90, 91
Bulletin of Atomic Scientists, 151
Burke, Edmund, 26, 27
Bush, Dr. Vannevar, 153

Cabinet Government, 108
Canonicus, Chief, 5
Carnegie, Mrs. Andrew, 141

Carranza, Venustiano, 111
Castro, Fidel, 165, 168
Catholic Church, 137
Chambers, John, Attorney General, 18
Chaney, James E., 84
Charles I, King, 7, 9
Charles II, King, 9
Chevalier, Haakon, 148, 149, 153
Christianity, xiii, 5, 6, 7, 30, 31
CIA, 157, 166–169
Civil Disobedience, 67, 73, 74
Civil War, 63, 83–84, 134
Clarke, George W., 83
Clarke, Governor George, 19
Clay, Henry, 58
Clayton Anti-Trust Act, 104
Clemenceau, Georges, 113–114
Cleveland, President Grover, 99
Clinton, Governor de Witt, 39
Coddington, William, 6, 8
Coke, Sir Edward, 2
Cold War, 150, 157, 160, 162, 167, 174, 175
Committee on Marriage and the Home, 142
Common Sense, 23, 24
Communism, 147, 162, 163, 168
Compton, Dr. Arthur, 148, 149
Compton, Karl, 146
Comstock, Anthony, 135
Conant, Dr. James, 150
Connally, Thomas, 118
Constitution, United States, 10, 20, 67
Constitutional Convention, 26

Continental Congress, 22, 24, 25
Copernicus, 74
Cosby, Governor William, 11–16, 18, 19
Cox, James M., 102, 118
Coyle, Capt. John, 33, 34
Crisis, The, 24–26
Cromwell, Oliver, 2, 7

Darrow, Clarence, 99
Davis, Jefferson, 51, 64, 65
Deane, Silas, 25, 26
Debs, Eugene, 95–105
Declaration of Independence, 23, 24, 45, 87
Defense Department, 154
De Gaulle, Charles, 154
Dennett, Mary Ware, 139
Dominican Republic invasion, 169
Dorret family, 36
Douglas, Stephen, 62, 116
Draft riots, 55
Dreiser, Theodore, 44
Dreyfus case, 154
Duke of Wellington, 89
Dulles, John Foster, 151, 164–165, 171, 172, 175

Eaton, Senator John, 34
Einstein, Albert, 141
Eisenhower, President Dwight, 147, 152, 155, 162, 163, 164, 166, 167, 168
Eliot, Harvard President, 128
Ellis, Havelock, 138
Eltenton, George, 148, 149, 153

Emancipation Proclamation, 63, 84
Emerson, Ralph Waldo, 51, 68–69, 73, 77
Espionage Act, 95
Evans, Dr. Ward V., 154, 155

Fall, Senator Albert, 116
Family Limitation, 138, 140
Fascism, 147, 148, 159
FBI, 152, 168
Fermi, Enrico, 148, 149, 150, 155
Firemen's Magazine, 96
Flanders, Senator Ralph, 163
Florence Crittenton Home, 128
Foreign Aid Program, 175
Fourierism, 59
Fourteen Points, 113–114
Franco, Francisco, 147
Franklin, Benjamin, 22, 64
Freedom Riders, 84
Fugitive Slave Act, 81
Fulbright, J. William, 157–176
Fulbright Scholarship Act, 161

Galileo, xiv
Galt, Edith Bolling, 112
Gandhi, Mahatma, 67, 77
Gavin, General James, 173
Gay, Sidney, 55
General Federation of Women's Clubs, 142
General Managers' Association, 98
Geneva Accords, 171, 172
George III, King, 22
Goldman, Emma, 141
Gompers, Samuel, 100

Goodman, Andrew, 84
Gordon, William, 24
Graham, Dr. Sylvester, 60
Grant, Ulysses S., 51, 65
Gray, Gordon, 152, 153, 154
Grayson, Dr. Gary, 113, 115
Great Northern Railroad, 97
Greeley, Horace, 44, 51, 55–66, 69, 72, 75, 76, 84, 88, 92
Greene, Gen. Nathaniel, 24
Groves, Gen. Leslie R., 153
Gulf of Tonkin Resolution, 169

Hamilton, Alexander, 45
Hamilton, Andrew, 16, 18, 19
Harding, President Warren G., 102, 104, 118
Harrison, President William Henry, 58, 88
Harte, Bret, 65
Hartke, Senator Vance, 173
Hawthorne, Nathaniel, 69
Hayes, Archbishop Patrick J., 137
Haywood, Big Bill, 101
Higgins, Margaret (*see* Sanger)
Hill, George, 123, 125, 126
Hill, Legrand, 123
Hillquit, Morris, 102
Hiroshima, 149
Hiss, Alger, 163
Hitler, Adolf, 147, 163
Ho Chi Minh, 170–172
Hooker, Thomas, 2, 4
House Foreign Affairs Committee, 159
Howe, General, 25

Huerta, Victoriano, 110, 111

Huntress, The, 41

Hutchinson, Anne, 6

Ibsen, Henrik, xiv

Industrial Workers of the World
(I.W.W.), 101

Ingersoll, Robert G., 134

Institute for Advanced Study,
Princeton, N.J., 151

International Atomic Energy
Commission, 152

Jackson, President Andrew, 39, 42,
51

James, Henry, 69

Jay, John, 64

Jefferson, Thomas, 24, 30, 35, 45

Jeffersonian, 58

Johnson, President Lyndon B., 145,
150, 157, 169, 172, 175

Joint Committee of Congress on
Atomic Energy, 152

Junior Leagues, 142

Kai-shek, Chiang, 166

Kennan, George, 173

Kennedy, President John, 145, 150,
158, 161, 167, 168, 169, 172

Khrushchev, Nikita, 166, 167, 168

King, Martin Luther, 67, 77

Korean War, 166

Krupp munitions, 101

Labor unions, 97, 100

Lansdale, Col. John, 149

Latin America, 110, 168, 175

League of Nations, 107, 113–114,
118

Lebanon invasion, 166

Lee, Robert E., 51

Lenin, Vladimir, 112

*Letters to the Citizens of the United
States*, 30

Lewis, Sinclair, 44

Lilienthal, David, 154

Lily, The, 88–89

Lincoln, President Abraham, 51,
60–64, 72, 84, 116

Lind, Jenny, 89

Lippmann, Walter, 139, 157

Lloyd George, 107, 108, 113–114

Lodge, Henry Cabot, 113–116, 118

Los Alamos, 145, 148, 149

Louis XVI, King, 25, 27, 28

Lovejoy, Elijah, 84

Lovejoy, Owen, 84

Luther, Martin, 74

McCarthy, Senator Joseph, 152,
153, 162, 163, 165

Madero, Francisco, 110

Malraux, Andre, 154

Manchester Guardian, 174

Manhattan District, 149

Marie Antoinette, 27

Marx, Karl, 62

Masham, Sir William, 2

Masonry, 39–40

Massasoit, Chief, 5

Mencken, H. L., 44

Mexican War, 60, 61

Miller, Mrs. Elizabeth Smith, 88,
   89, 91
Milton, John, 7
Monroe, James, 29, 36
Morgan affair, 40
Morris, Governor, 20, 24
Morris, Lewis, 13, 14
Morse, Samuel, 42
Morse, Senator Wayne, 163
Mussolini, Benito, 147, 163

Nagasaki, 149
National Academy of Science, 153
National Birth Control League, 136,
   137, 139
National Council of Jewish Women,
   142
National Defense Council, 167
National Defense Research
   Committee, 150
Negroes, 55, 67, 74, 82, 84, 100,
   175
New York County Medical Society,
   142
New York Gazette, 12, 14
New York Herald, 87
New York Penal Code, 131, 140
New York Society for Suppression of
   Vice, 135
New York Sun, 59
New York Times, 86, 157
New York Tribune, 55–65, 76, 92,
   117
New York Weekly Journal, 11, 14
New Yorker, The, 56, 58, 59
Nuclear weapons, 155, 157

Oak Ridge, 148
Olney, Richard, 98
Oppenheimer, Dr. J. Robert,
   145–155
Organization of American States
   (OAS), 170
Orlando, Count Vittorio, 114
Owens, Dr. Bethenia, 121–130

Paine, Thomas, 21–31, 35
Palmer, Dr., 121–122, 126, 127
Palmer, Joseph, 45–53
Paul Pry, 41
Pauling, Dr. Linus, 146
Pennsylvania Magazine, 22, 23
Pershing, Gen. John, 111
Physical Review, 146
Pierce, President Franklin, 35, 43
Pitt, William, 27
Planned Parenthood, 131–143
Planned Parenthood Federation of
   America, 142
Polk, President James K., 60, 61
Princeton University, 108, 151
Pullman Company, 97
Pullman, George, 97

Randolph, John, 38
Raymond, Henry, 62
Red China, 166, 170, 172, 174
*Reflections on the Revolution in
   France*, 26
Reform dress, 92, 93
Revolution, American, 27–29, 31,
   36

Revolution, French, 26–27
Rights of Man, The, 26, 27
Robespierre, Maximilien, 29
Rock, Dr. John, 142
Rockefeller, Mrs. John D., 141
Roosevelt, Franklin D., 159, 162
Roosevelt, Theodore, 100, 109, 110, 113
Royall, Anne, 33–44
Royall, Capt. William, 35
Russell, Bertrand, 141

Salisbury, Lady, 89
Sanger, Margaret, 131–143
Sanger, William, 135, 136
Schwerner, Michael, 84
Seminole Indian War, 81
Senate Foreign Relations
    Committee, 113, 157, 162, 166, 171, 173, 174
Seneca City Courier, 87
Seward, William, 58, 62, 63
Sinclair, Upton, 44
Sketches of History, Life and Manners in the United States, 36
Slee, J. Noah H., 141
Smith, Gerrit, 88
Smith, Margaret Chase, 170
Smyth, Dr. Henry DeWolf, 152, 154, 155
Socialism, 59, 99, 101, 102, 104, 105
Socialist Call, 135
Spanish Civil War, 147
Stalin, Joseph, 147, 160, 163, 166

Stanton, Mrs. Elizabeth Cady, 87–89, 91
Stone, Lucy, 89, 91
Strikes, 97–100
Symes, Sheriff John, 11, 12, 15
Szilard, Leo, 146, 149

Taft, William Howard, 109
Taylor, Zachary, 61
Teller, Dr. Edward, 151
Temperance, 51, 87, 88, 90, 93
Thomas, Father John L., 137
Thomas, Norman, 104
Thoreau, Henry David, 44, 67–77, 96, 176
Thoreau, Maria, 73
Tocqueville, Alexis de, 87
Trask, Rev. George, 46
Treason, 163
Truman, President Harry S., 146, 149, 159, 160, 161
Trusts, 100, 110
Tumulty, Joseph, 103, 112
Twain, Mark, 65

U-2 spy plane, 166, 167
United Nations, 118, 159–161, 166, 174, 175
United Nations Atomic Energy
    Commission, 149
United States Atomic Energy
    Commission, 145, 146, 149, 154, 155
United States-Soviet relations, 148–151, 160, 164–168

Van Buren, Martin, 35
Van Dam, Rip, 13–14
Vanema's Arithmetica, 13
Versailles Treaty, 113
Vietnam War, 61, 72, 77, 105,
     169–175
Villa, Pancho, 111

Wagner National Labor Relations
     Act, 62, 104
Walden, 70
Walker, Jonathan, 79–84
Watterson, Henry, 33
Weed, Thurlow, 57, 58, 61–63
Welch, Joseph N., 165
Wells, H. G., 139, 141
Western Federation of Miners, 101
Western Home Visitor, 92
Whalen, Grover, 142
What Every Girl Should Know, 135
Whitman, Walt, 51
Whitman, Dr. Walter G., 154
Whittier, John Greenleaf, 83, 84
Williams, Roger, 1–10, 20, 38, 41
Wilson, Charles E., 152
Wilson, Edith, 116
Wilson, Ellen, 108, 111
Wilson, President Woodrow, 100,
     101, 107–119
Woman Rebel, The, 136–138
Women's Rights Convention, 87, 89
Women's suffrage, 66, 88, 93
Wood, Mayor Fernando, 55
World Council of Churches, 170,
     173
World Population Conference, 141

World War I, 95, 112
World War II, 115, 118, 176

Zaharoff, Basil, 101
Zenger, John Peter, 11–20